What's left of
HENRY VIII

DEBORAH JAFFÉ

from Deborah November 1995

DIAL
HOUSE

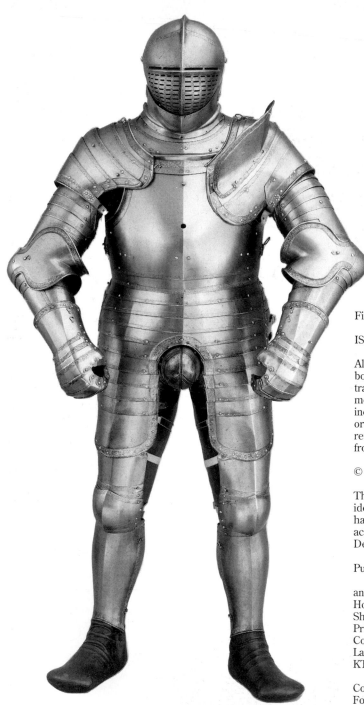

First published 1995

ISBN 0 7110 2304 2

© 1995 Deborah Jaffé

The right of Deborah Jaffé to be
identified as the Author of this work
has been asserted by her in
accordance with the Copyrights,
Designs and Patents Act 1988.

Published by Dial House

an imprint of Ian Allan Ltd, Terminal
House, Station Approach,
Shepperton, Surrey TW17 8AS.
Printed by Ian Allan Printing Ltd,
Coombelands House, Coombelands
Lane, Addlestone, Weybridge, Surrey
KT15 1HY.

Cover: Hampton Court. *Aerofilms*
Fountains Abbey. *AA Picture Library*
Henry VIII. *National Portrait Gallery*

CONTENTS

Left:
Mary, who succeeded Henry VIII to the throne in 1553.
From the collection of Dulwich Picture Gallery, London, on loan to Tredegar House.

Acknowledgements

Many people have given me information, ideas and theories about Henry VIII and this book. I would like to thank them all especially: Dickie Arbiter, Royal Collection Enterprises; Richard Coxon, The Crown Estate; Colin Dunston; Mandy Little and Sheila Watson; Peter Waller; Celia Stern, of the Photo Library and Kim Robbins of the Press Office, English Heritage; Christina Mackwell, Lambeth Palace Library; Linda Tilbury, Lincoln Cathedral; Deirdre Mortimer, York Minster Library; the staff of the Public Information Office, House of Commons; The staff of the Photo Library, The National Trust; The staff, Department of Coins and Medals, British Museum; the staff of the Public Record Office, Chancery Lane; the staff of the London Library; the many site representatives, information and publicity managers, and curators throughout the country who have responded enthusiastically to requests for information, no matter how obscure. Finally, thanks to Elizabeth Duff for her excellent proof-reading, comments and source of information about midwifery; to Tricia Oakley Kessler who provided many thought-provoking insights; to my mother Mavis Jaffé for her continued interest in the development of the book; to my husband George Kessler for his interest, support and endless discussions on philosophy; and lastly to my daughters, Madeleine and Flora Kessler who, through their questions and drawings, created their own relationship with Henry VIII.

To Madeleine and Flora

INTRODUCTION

Researching this book has been both fascinating and gruesome. The fascination lay in the endless sources of information about Henry VIII and his times and the links they have with our lives today. There is, however, the macabre aspect when dealing with a man such as Henry. The infliction of horrors was never too great in the pursuit of goals. This highly cultured man, who became increasingly power crazed, was, like many other dictators before and since, both charming and ruthless.

There is much more to Henry VIII than the endless jokes about his sexual prowess and six wives. His impact on English life has been enormous and in many respects the story of his activities is still relevant today. Without him the Church of England might never have been created and the countryside could be full of beautifully kept monastic buildings instead of ruins. Coins still bear the 'FD' in recognition of the monarch being Defender of the Faith, a title bestowed on Henry in 1521 by Pope Leo X. Henry was the first monarch to be head of the church in England. Politically, Europe continues to be divided; like Henry we try to make uneasy links with European allies. There are still wars between Christians and Muslims as there were between Christendom and the Ottoman Empire in the 16th century. Although Scotland and England are part of Britain, nationalism is not forgotten.

Everyone living in Britain has consciously and subliminally been influenced by Henry VIII and his regime. The aim of this book is to introduce readers to the enormity of this influence and give them the opportunity to experience Henry in their own ways. An actor recently described how valuable it was to stand in one of Henry's many houses, to look out of the window and at the floor and to listen to sounds, in preparation for playing the part. So it has been in writing this book: by finding his gloves, armour, portraits, coat of arms, houses and forts, by contemplating the magnitude of his political and cultural changes, Henry became much more than another character in a history book.

Left:
Henry's second daughter, the result of his marriage to Anne Boleyn, was Elizabeth. She succeeded Mary to the throne in 1558 and over a long reign successfully held the country together. This portrait of her, by John Bettes the Younger, shows the Queen towards the end of her life.
© *Hever Castle Ltd*

Site Information

Whilst information about opening times and admission charges were correct at the time of going to press, changes do occur. Many sites are open all year, others only in summer. Bank Holiday opening is now popular whilst some places are closed every Monday; the variation in opening times is enormous, so please do telephone beforehand and check to avoid disappointment.

Whilst every effort has been made to ensure the accuracy of the information contained within this book, neither the Publisher nor the Author can accept any liability arising from its use. Users are recommended to verify personally that sites are open prior to undertaking a visit. It should also be stressed that displays at museums and country houses can change and that items within a collection may not always be available for public display.

NB: Site information is provided throughout this book under the following categories:
1. **Opening times**
2. **Admission charges**
3. **Parking**

CHAPTER 1:
CHRONOLOGY OF
EVENTS DURING
HENRY VIII'S REIGN

1485	Battle of Bosworth Field, Richard III killed and Henry Tudor becomes King Henry VII.
1486	Marriage of Henry VII and Elizabeth of York.
1486	Birth of Arthur, Prince of Wales.
1488	Treaty between England and Castile for the future marriage of Prince Arthur and Catherine of Aragon.
1489	Birth of Margaret (who eventually marries James V of Scotland).
1491	Birth of Henry at Greenwich (28 June)
1493	Henry made Constable of Dover Castle, Warden of the Cinque Ports and Earl Marshal of England (5 April)
1494	Henry created Lord Lieutenant of Ireland, Knight of the Bath, Duke of York and Lord Warden of the Marches of Scotland.
1495	Henry made a Knight of the Garter.
1496	Birth of Mary (known later as the French Queen after which she marries Charles Brandon, Duke of Suffolk).
1499	Henry's first meeting with Thomas More and Desiderius Erasmus.
1501	Catherine of Aragon arrives in Plymouth. Arthur and Catherine marry at St Paul's Cathedral (14 November)
1502	Arthur dies at Ludlow. Henry becomes Duke of Cornwall. Treaty to allow marriage of Catherine to Henry.

Previous page:
Henry VII and Henry VIII, part of the cartoon drawn by Holbein in 1536, which included Elizabeth of York, Jane Seymour and Edward.
© *National Portrait Gallery, London*

Below:
Chronology of some of Henry VIII's contemporaries

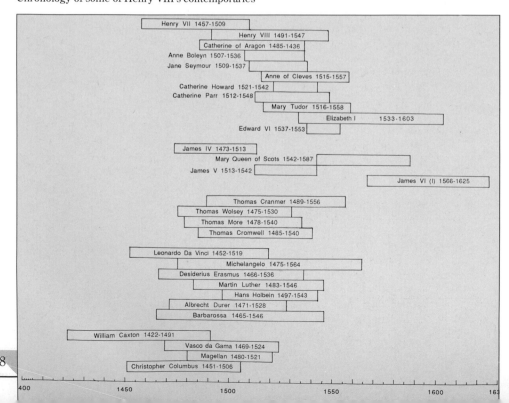

1503	Death of Elizabeth of York, buried in Westminster Abbey. Henry created Prince of Wales. Pope grants dispensation to annul marriage of Arthur and Catherine.
1509	Death of Henry VII at Richmond, buried in Westminster Abbey. Accession of Henry as King Henry VIII of England, France and Ireland. Marriage of Henry to Catherine of Aragon in Greenwich (11 June). Coronation in Westminster Abbey (24 June).
1509	Henry considers going to war with France, encouraged by the Pope.
1510	Catherine has a still-born daughter. Dudley and Empson beheaded on Tower Hill.
1511	Catherine gives birth to a son, Henry, who dies at seven weeks. Henry's adultery begins.
1511	Thomas Wolsey, Dean of Lincoln, becomes a member of King's Council. Henry and Ferdinand of Spain agree to go to war with France.
1512	Henry sends 7,000 men to Spain. Ferdinand wants Navarre for Spain and does not take Aquitaine for Henry as agreed. Soldiers mutiny. English fight French navy off Brest and lose 'The Regency'.
1513	Henry plans another invasion of France with 60,000 men and leaves Dover for Calais with a fleet of 300 ships. Erasmus wants diplomatic peace, Thomas More is anti-French and John Colet, Dean of St Paul's, denounces war. James IV allies with France in the war and his soldiers cross the border at Coldstream. Tournai falls to Henry. Battle of Flodden. James IV killed and Scotland defeated. French surrender. James V, age 17 months, now King of Scotland, Margaret, Henry's sister, acts as regent. 1514 New peers created in respect of victories: Earl of Surrey becomes Duke of Norfolk, his son, Lord Thomas Howard is Earl of Surrey, Charles Brandon becomes Duke of Suffolk and his title, Viscount Lisle, passes to Arthur Plantagenet. Thomas Wolsey becomes Bishop of Lincoln and Tournai. Brandon, Duke of Suffolk, becomes interested in Henry's sister Mary. She marries Louis XII and is known as 'The French Queen'. Henry prepares to invade France again.
1515	Louis XII dies. Mary marries Suffolk secretly. Accession of François I of France. The Virgin Mary, known as The Mary Rose, warship launched at Woolwich. Wolsey made a Cardinal and replaces Warham as Lord Chancellor.
1516	Ferdinand of Spain dies, succeeded by his grandson, Charles. Queen Catherine gives birth to a daughter, Mary. Mary and Suffolk have a son who becomes Earl of Lincoln. Henry makes an alliance with Maximilian and Charles.
1517	Uprising in London stopped by Henry, Wolsey and More. Martin Luther nails 95 theses to a church door in Wittenberg, Germany.
1518	Henry sells Tournai to France. Pope wants a unified Christendom against the Turk. Catherine has a still-born daughter. Henry has an affair with Elizabeth Blount.
1519	Elizabeth Blount gives birth to Henry's son, Lord Harry Fitzroy.
1520	Field of the Cloth of Gold. Earl of Surrey appointed Deputy of Ireland to quell unrest. Border troubles with Scotland at Tynedale and Resedale.
1521	Buckingham arrested for treason and beheaded on Tower Hill. Beginning of the Great Enterprise. Henry writes Assertion of the Seven Sacraments, opposing Luther's teachings. Pope pleased with the book and gives Henry and his successors title, 'Defender of the Faith'.
1522	Charles V visits England and agrees to marry Mary, Henry's daughter, when she is 14 years old. François faced with an allied enemy of England, The Holy Roman Empire, the Pope, and Italian and Swiss states.

	Skirmishes on border with Scotland.
523	Thomas More writes *Answer to Luther*.
1524	War with France continues. François held prisoner, Henry wants to invade France and become king but Charles does not allow it.
1525	Charles wants part of Mary's dowry and her to come to Spain. Marriage contract broken. Wolsey reaches agreement with French ambassador. Henry tries to break the alliance between France and Scotland. Cambridge academics begin to follow Luther. Illegal publication of William Tyndale's translation, into English, of the New Testament, immediately declared a heresy. Dissent from the population about paying taxes to support foreign policy and wars. Wolsey, the Papal Legate, begins to suppress monasteries to fund new colleges at Oxford and Ipswich. Henry has a new mistress, Mary Boleyn (Anne's sister) from Hever Castle. He considers divorcing Catherine in his quest for a son.
1526	The painter Hans Holbein the Younger arrives in London.
1527	Henry hostile to Charles V, Catherine's nephew. He starts divorce proceedings against her, she informs Charles. Henry falls in love with Anne Boleyn. Wolsey is not in favour of the divorce.
1528	High taxes, a poor summer and food shortages provoke unrest. Possibility of a war with the Netherlands means no wool exports from England. Riots in Westbury, Taunton, Bridgwater and Colchester. Workers in Kent villages march to Knole, Warham's Palace. Divorce proceedings publicised.
1529	Court proceedings begin. Wolsey's term ends. Sir Thomas More becomes Lord Chancellor. Cardinal's College, founded by Wolsey, becomes King Henry VIII's College, Oxford.
1530	More does not sign documents asking Pope for a divorce. Wolsey charged with high treason, dies at Leicester Abbey on his way to the Tower.
1531	Thomas Cromwell joins the court. Persecution of heretics. Henry publishes *The Glass of the Truth*. Anne Boleyn now publicly Henry's mistress. They go on a progress together. Henry and Catherine meet for the last time.
1532	Sir Thomas More resigns. Sir Thomas Audley becomes Lord Chancellor. Soleiman the Magnificent plans to invade Austria. Henry refuses to support Charles and sides with François, which helps to keep the peace on Scottish border. Warham dies, Cranmer becomes Archbishop of Canterbury. Anne Boleyn is made Marquess of Pembroke. Henry and Anne meet François in Boulogne to discuss the future of Christendom.
1533	Mary, the French Queen, Henry's sister, dies aged 37 years. Anne announces she is pregnant, they rush to make it legitimate so she and Henry marry in secret around 25 January. Final break with Rome. Henry called 'Your Majesty', the first English monarch to be so. He was ruler of his own land with no one between him and God. Cranmer becomes Archbishop of Canterbury at St Stephen's Westminster. He declares Henry and Catherine's marriage was unlawful, allowing them both to remarry. Anne crowned in Westminster Abbey. Henry demands Catherine is no longer called 'Queen' but 'Dowager Princess of Wales' and Mary, their daughter, is declared illegitimate because her parent's marriage was unlawful. He wants her to be 'The King's daughter, Lady Mary'. Both refuse. Birth of Elizabeth, the daughter of Henry and Anne Boleyn and the future Elizabeth I. Henry moves Catherine to Buckden, Huntingdon, and makes Mary Lady in Waiting to Elizabeth.

1534	An Act of Parliament makes Henry Supreme Head of the Church in England establishing royal, not Papal, supremacy. Pope states the marriage between Henry and Catherine was legal, Henry ignores him. All Papal references have to be removed from prayer books. Oath of Allegiance passed by Parliament, whereby clergy and others swear allegiance to king, queen and their children, not to God. Treason to deny this. Executions of Papists, Anabaptists and heretics. Catherine and Mary refuse to sign the Oath. James V of Scotland supports Catherine. Troubles in Ireland. The prelate John Fisher made a Papal Cardinal.
1535	Thomas Cromwell becomes Vicar General making him, a layman, more powerful than the archbishops and bishops. Fisher beheaded for treason. Sir Thomas More beheaded at Tower Hill. Henry stays at Sir John Seymour's home, Wolf Hall in Savernake Forest. His daughter Jane is 26 years old. Anne is pregnant again. Act passed to allow domination of Ireland. Plans for the suppression of the monasteries begin. Henry considers making England Lutheran.
1536	Queen Catherine dies at Kimbolton and is buried in Peterborough Cathedral (January). Henry attempts to rebuild the relationship with Spain. Anne has a miscarriage, Henry pursues Jane Seymour. Ten Articles published, everyone had to believe in them. Split amongst orthodox and progressive bishops. Reginald Pole, Henry's cousin, is outspoken against his tyranny. The Pope makes him a Cardinal whilst Henry calls him a traitor to England. Rumours spread of Anne's adultery with five men, including her brother, who all go to the Tower and are executed. Cranmer grants a dispensation before she dies leaving Henry free to marry Jane Seymour, making Elizabeth illegitimate. Henry and Jane Seymour marry (30 May). Mary refuses to swear allegiance to Henry. He threatens to execute her. Wales divided into counties. Welsh customs suppressed and English spoken. The Pilgrimage of Grace, an uprising, in the north, against the dissolution of the monasteries and new religious laws. Henry has to grant pardons to all rebels living north of Doncaster.
1537	Jane Seymour is pregnant. Henry's health begins to deteriorate and he gains weight. The Duke of Richmond, Henry's illegitimate son, by Elizabeth Blount, dies aged 17 years. Bishops accept Luther's Confession of Augsburg of three sacraments. Cromwell allows the Ten Articles to be produced and enforced on everyone. The Bible is published in English and distributed to churches. Jane Seymour gives birth (12 October), by Caesarean section, to Edward at Hampton Court. She dies ten days later and is buried at Windsor. Holbein is sent to paint the Duchess of Milan and Louise of Guise. James V marries Mary of Guise. Desecration by Henry's troops of shrines at Walsingham, Chichester and Canterbury (St Thomas à Becket's). Pope excommunicates Henry because of desecration of shrines. Europe against England. Henry considers marrying Anne of Cleves, a German Lutheran.
1539	Warships arrive in Margate from Flushing, people called to defend England, those who refuse are arrested. Six Articles of Religion passed, those who disagreed are executed as traitors. Duke of Cleves signs a treaty for marriage between his sister Anne and Henry. Holbein is sent to paint her. Anne of Cleves travels from Düsseldorf to Dover via Calais (December)

1540	Anne and Henry meet at Shooters Hill. She was not as pretty as he had imagined. They marry, do not consummate the marriage and divorce five months later. Henry falls in love with Katherine Howard, Norfolk's niece. Cromwell declared to be a false and corrupt traitor and is kept in the Tower until Henry divorces Anne of Cleves. Cromwell beheaded. Henry marries Katherine Howard. All monasteries now suppressed, it has taken four years and hundreds of lives.
1541	Henry becomes King of Ireland. Henry and Katherine go to York. During the visit Katherine continues her earlier affair with Culpepper. Cranmer informs Henry of her adultery, she is imprisoned at Syon House. Culpepper and Dereham (another lover) are executed.
1542	Katherine beheaded at Tower Green (February). Scottish border raids between Kelso and Jedburgh. Eccles and Kelso are burnt but the Scots win. 18,000 Scots cross the border at Gretna. Battle at Solway Moss, Henry announces Scotland as his and wants Mary Queen of Scots, eventually to marry Prince Edward.
1543	Henry marries Katherine Parr, then aged 31 (July). Scots refuse to give Mary Queen of Scots to Henry and revolt.
1544	Henry orders Suffolk to plunder and burn Edinburgh. Charles and Henry decide to invade France. Henry's troops take Boulogne. Henry goes to France to take control of the army, against everyone's wishes, and finds himself at war with both François and Charles.
1545	Scottish border troubles. French navy in the Channel and 2,000 French soldiers in Scotland. François wants Boulogne back. Henry dines on the *Mary Rose* and later watches her sink. He does not want to return to Boulogne nor for it to be part of a peace deal with Scotland. Cranmer accused of heresy but released before going to Tower.
1546	Fighting between French and English at St Etiennne. Peace signed at Campagne-les-Guisnes. Scottish border troubles continue. Anti-Protestant purges led by Lord Chancellor Wriothesley, on Henry's orders. Henry gets worried by Katherine's Protestantism, he considers sending her to the Tower. Norfolk and his son and Anne Askew, a reformer, are sent to the Tower.
1547	Surrey beheaded on Tower Hill. Norfolk ordered to be hung, drawn and quartered. Henry is very ill. Cranmer is sent for and is his last confessor (27 January). Henry dies at 2am (28 January). His death is kept secret for a few days. Prince Edward proclaimed King Edward VI (31 January). Norfolk reprieved but remains in Tower.

CHAPTER 2:
HENRY VIII

W hen he died in 1547, aged 56, Henry VIII had been King of England and France for 38 years. During that time England underwent one of the most major periods of transformation in its history and Henry was the instigator of irrevocable change.

He was the second son of Henry VII (Henry Tudor) and Elizabeth of York. Their eldest son Arthur, Prince of Wales, was born heir to the throne but died long before his father. Henry, the second son, was made Constable of Dover Castle, Warden of the Cinque Ports, and, whilst still a child, became Duke of Cornwall on his brother's death.

Like all European monarchs, Henry VII regarded marriage as a political alliance between two nations and in 1488 he signed a treaty with King Ferdinand of Aragon by which Arthur would marry the Spanish princess, Catherine. This would ensure a firm alliance between England and Aragon and Castile (kingdoms of Spain at that time) as Catherine's mother was Queen of Castile.

Catherine arrived at Plymouth in 1501 and married Arthur at St Paul's Cathedral later in the year. However, Arthur was only 16 when he died at Ludlow Castle in 1502 and whether this marriage had been consummated or not was to be the source of fierce argument years later.

After Arthur's death, another treaty was signed to allow a marriage to take place between Henry, now the heir, and the widowed Catherine. They married in 1509, only weeks after the death of Henry VII, and remained so for 24 years until their acrimonious divorce and the split with Rome. They were King and Queen of England, France, (which was the area around Calais) and Ireland. They were both Catholic and the Pope, in Rome, was head of the church.

The young king was handsome, slim and cultured. He was aware of European events and wanted England to be part of them. In Thomas Wolsey he had a loyal and invaluable Lord Chancellor who knew how to handle the running of the state and its European neighbours. This left Henry free to spend his days hunting whilst Wolsey ran the day-to-day affairs, although Henry made all the final decisions, on advice from Wolsey. Together they made a formidable partnership, plotting and scheming their way in and out of wars and disagreements with France and Scotland, and gradually with Rome.

Henry, having been well educated, spoke fluent Latin and French, composed music, wrote numerous books and was the founder of several schools. He took over the Cardinal's College, Oxford, founded by Wolsey, and made it King Henry VIII's College, now Christ Church. He then founded Trinity College Cambridge and the Cambridge University Press. He also became the greatest royal builder of all time, establishing palaces at Nonsuch, St James's and Whitehall and instigating new building projects at Windsor and Hampton Court. Henry later became even more wealthy with the land and effects he acquired from dissolved monasteries. Other houses were acquired on the demise of their owners (usually his advisers), notably Hampton Court from Wolsey and Penshurst Place from Buckingham.

London and the surrounding area, with the palaces, parliament and the Thames, was Henry's main base. He grew up at Eltham and Greenwich, built St James' Palace, Whitehall and Nonsuch and as the reign progressed spent more time at Richmond and Hampton Court. Like many monarchs and heads of state, Henry was keen to impress – especially foreign dignitaries. He based Nonsuch on the newly built Fontainebleau which had been influenced by designs

HENRIE

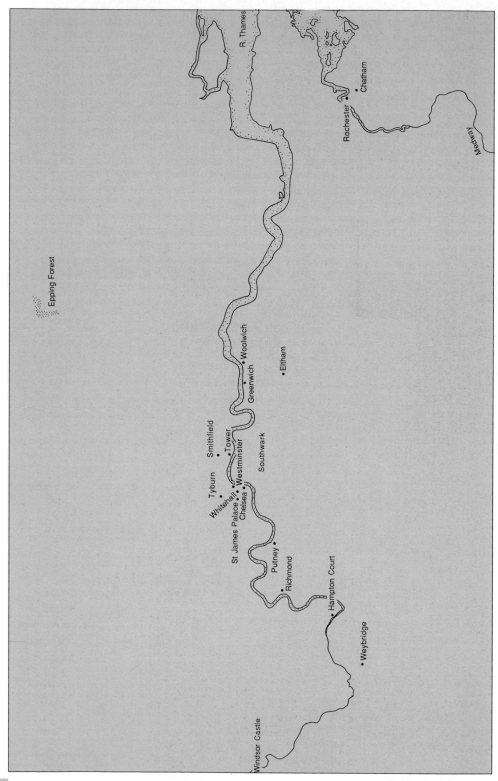

Epping Forest

R. Thames

Chatham
Rochester

Medway

Woolwich

Eltham

Greenwich

Smithfield

Tyburn
Tower
Westminster
Whitehall
St James Palace
Chelsea

Southwark

Putney
Richmond

Hampton Court

Weybridge

Windsor Castle

from Renaissance Florence. The Tower of London was used both as a royal residence and a prison.

In the summer the king and queen and their courts would escape the heat and risk of disease in the city by embarking on a 'progress'. A progress might take six weeks and was a major event as the court and servants made their way to six or seven different locations. Places like Enfield, Ampthill, Woking and Esher were all visited by Henry on his progress.

He also made frequent pilgrimages to the tomb of Thomas à Becket in Canterbury Cathedral, especially on his way to Calais via Dover.

Like many people with power, Henry became obsessive in his belief that he could achieve whatever he wished. For example, his desperate need for a divorce from Catherine, in order to marry Anne Boleyn in 1533, drove him to use his position for purely selfish gain. As Jasper Ridley writes, 'No statesman has been more aware than Henry VIII that politics is the art of the possible.'[1]

The drift into dictatorial madness involved the executions of two wives and the divorce of another two; suppression and dissolution of hundreds of monasteries and abbeys; pogroms and purges of heretics, Catholics and Lutherans alike; and England's isolation from the rest of Europe. The charming, cultured young man became a schemer unable to trust anyone. He felt his goal was justified no matter what the cost along the way; this was well described by Machiavelli in *The Prince*[2] and is assumed to be based on Henry VIII's activities.

In many respects his is a modern tale as we look at the world today and witness similar purges and wars, usually based on religious belief, personal power and non-understanding of the individual which are still costing untold lives.

[1]Jasper Ridley, *Henry VIII* , Constable 1992
[2]Niccolo Machiavelli, *The Prince*, Penguin Classics, Translation 1981

Left:
Vase of Venetian glass with an enamelled portrait of King Henry V11. Venice *circa* 1500.
© *British Museum*

Opposite:
Map showing the location of Henry VIII's principal buildings along the Thames

A View of RICHMOND PALACE fronting the River Thames, as built by King Henry VII.

Places to Visit

The National Portrait Gallery
See page 71.

The British Museum
Great Russell Street
London WC1B 3DG
0171 580 1788
1 All year
2 No
3 No
Room 46 at the British Museum houses a broad collection of artefacts from 15th- and 16th-century England. There is a roundel bearing Henry's coat of arms, coins and medals, a pilgrim's bottle, Holbein's designs for gift rolls and royal plate, an astrolabe and various pieces of silver. Henry's untidy, illegible handwriting is on display in the King's Library. Next to it is the elegant, neat and clearly legible writing of his daughter Elizabeth. Cromwell's notes relating to Catherine of Aragon and the Oath of Allegiance are also here.

Museum of London
London Wall
London EC2Y 5HN
0171 600 0807
1 All year, closed Mon
2 Yes
3 No
The Museum of London is the local museum of the 'square mile' around which much of Henry's life revolved but which was destroyed in the Great Fire of 1666. However, the museum has extensive displays recreating Tudor London, the merchants, religious life, and of course Henry VIII. There is also archaeological material from Nonsuch Palace.

Victoria and Albert Museum
Cromwell Road
South Kensington
London SW7 2RL
0171 938 8550
1 All year
2 Donation
3 No
The V&A's extensive Tudor Galleries include a vast collection of tapestries, embroidery, clothing, woodcarvings, silverware and room settings from the period. Among them is Henry VIII's writing desk and a pair of gauntlets, thought to be his.

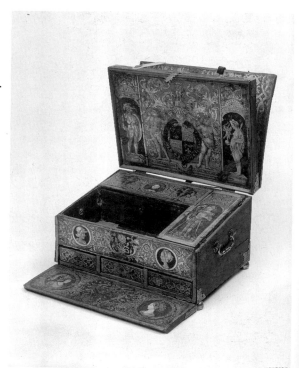

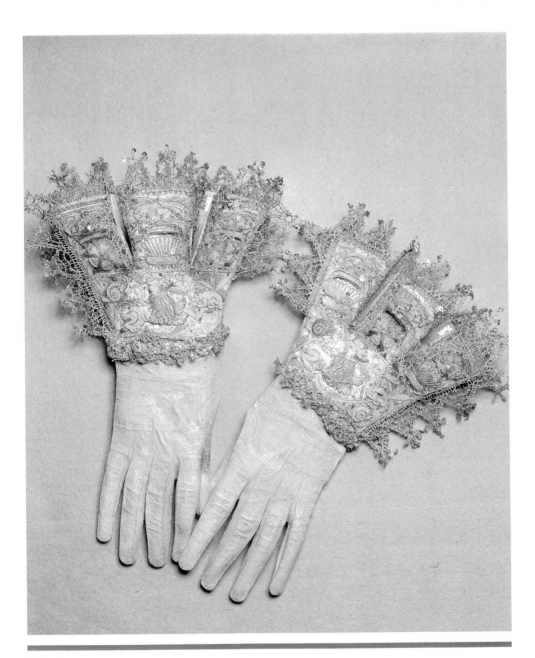

Opposite:
Amongst the various Tudor items on display at the Victoria & Albert Museum in London is this English writing desk of 1520. It is made of oak and walnut and is covered with gilt and painted decoration.
Courtesy of the Trustees of the V&A/Photographer: P. Barnard

Above:
A pair of 16th century leather gloves with gauntlets embroidered with silver-gilt and silver thread from the collection at the Victoria & Albert Museum.
Courtesy of the Trustees of the V&A

THE EAST VIEW OF KING HENRY VII PALACE, ON RICHMOND GREEN.

To the R.t Hon.ble GEORGE, Earl of Cholmondeley Visc.t Malpas, Baron Cholmondely of Wichmilbank, & Baron Newburgh Visc.t Kells, & Baron Hemborough of the Kingdom of Ireland, Chancellor of the Dutchy of Lancaster, Chamberlain, Lord Lieutenant Custos Rotulorum & Vice Admiral of the County Palatine of Chester, Governor of the Castle & City of Chester, Lord Lieut.t of the several Counties in N.th Wales, Knight of the most Hon.ble Order of the Bath, & one of his Majesties most Hon.ble Privy Council.
This Prospect is most humbly Inscrib'd by his Lordships most Obed.t Serv.t Sam.l & Nath.l Buck.

RICHMOND anciently call'd Shene or Shine from its Beauty has always been in great Estimation for y.e Purity of its Air, & was formerly much frequented by our Princes. Here died K.g Edw.rd III of Grief & displeasure of his Son y.e Black Prince. Here also departed those Daughters of y.e Emperor Charles IV & Consort of K.g Edw.rd III whose Death that Prince took so much at Heart that he caused y.e Palace to be laid in Ruins. K.g Hen.y V rendered it. In K.g Hen. VII Time it was reduced to Ashes by an accidental fire, but by that Prince it was raised again, to a State of Magnificence much superior to any thing had been here seen before, & call'd Richmond from y.e Title he bore while a Subject, t'was scarce finisht when in it he Breath'd his last. Here likewise died Q. Elizabeth. Sam.l & Nath.l Buck del. & sculp. Pub.d & sold according to the of Parliament March 25.th 1739.

PALATIVM REGIVM IN ANGLIÆ REGNO APPELLATVM NONCIVTZ,
Hoc est nusquam simile.

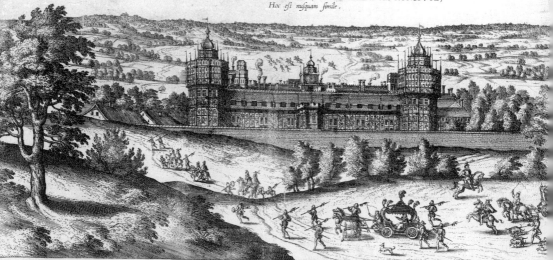

Effigiauit Georgius Houfnaglius Anno 1582.

Anglia   Serratorum uxores   Nobiles mulieres Anglicæ   Perampinus

22

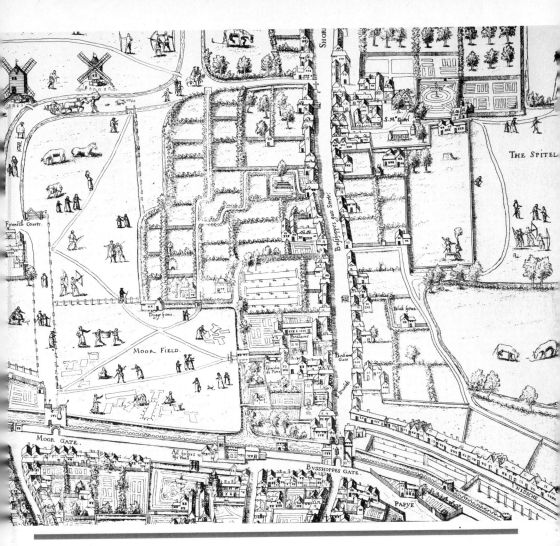

Above opposite:
The east view of the Palace at Richmond.
The Fotomas Index

Opposite:
A late 16th century view of Nonsuch Palace.
The Fotomas Index

Above:
A copperplate map of the Moorfields area, north of the city, *circa* 1558, at the Museum of London. This
shows the nature of part of the Tudor capital with its surviving city walls. The Moor Gate and the
Bishop's Gate are today part of the City of London's financial hub; Finsbury (Fynnesburie) and
Shoreditch (Shordiche) lie on its perimeter.
© *Museum of London*

Following page:
The Imperial State Crown was made for the coronation of George VI in 1937. However many of the jewels
contained in it date from pre-Tudor times. It is thought that the drop-shaped pearls were passed from
Catherine de Medici to her daughter-in-law, Mary, Queen of Scots. On her execution they were sold to
Elizabeth I.
© *Historic Royal Palaces*

The Public Record Office
(Good Reference Libraries)
Chancery Lane
London WC2A 1LR
0181 876 3444
1 All year
2 No
3 No
Henry VIII is the best documented of all monarchs. The Public Record Office and reference libraries hold 21 volumes of 'Letters and Papers, Foreign and Domestic of the Reign of Henry VIII' and 11 volumes of the 'State Papers of Henry VIII.' These have been transcribed into modern English and are fascinating to read. There are guest lists for his Coronation; letters from Henry and Catherine of Aragon to her father proclaiming their love and happiness; lists of rents accrued by Catherine from properties inherited from Prince Arthur; notes to Wolsey and Cromwell; reports of surveyors' visits to monasteries, the activities of the monks and property valuations; inventories of wardrobes and rooms at Henry's death and plans for his funeral. These documents are all informative and reveal the breadth of Henry's influence and activities.

HM Tower of London
Tower Hill Pageant
1 Tower Hill Terrace
London EC3N 4EE
0171 709 0081
1 All year
2 Yes
3 No
The Pageant takes you on a ride through the history of the City of London from AD50 to 1994 (see pages 45, 102 and 147).

ho: Moor L.ᵈChancelour

CHAPTER 3: INFLUENTIAL CHARACTERS

John Fisher 1469–1535

The scholar John Fisher had long been associated with the courts of Henry VII and Henry VIII, becoming Chancellor of Cambridge University and Bishop of Rochester. He strongly opposed Luther, was held in high esteem by Henry and became confessor to Catherine of Aragon. However, his fate was sealed by his opposition to the divorce proceedings, going to all lengths to prove the validity of the marriage. In 1531 he refused to accept the Act of Supremacy. He was imprisoned in the Tower with his friend, Sir Thomas More, and executed in June 1535. The Pope, to add to Henry's fury, made him a Papal Cardinal a few days before his death. His head preceded More's on the railings of Tower Bridge. Fisher was canonised in 1935 and shares his feast day, 22 June, with More.

Sir Thomas More 1478–1535

Sir Thomas More is the best-known of Henry's Lord Chancellors. The son of a judge, he joined the Archbishop of Canterbury's staff when he was 13 years old, studied at Oxford University, entered Lincoln's Inn, was called to the Bar in 1501 and later became a Member of Parliament. For a number of years he considered becoming a priest but decided to marry instead. However, in respect of his religious leanings, he always wore a hair shirt.

Henry recognised More's talents and breadth of interest and quickly promoted him. He was made Under-Sheriff of London, 1510; envoy to Flanders, 1516; Privy Councillor and Master of Requests, 1518; Speaker of the House of Commons, 1523; High Steward of Oxford University, 1524; High Steward of Cambridge University and Chancellor of the Duchy of Lancaster, 1525. He was the first Speaker of the House of Commons to make a request for free speech.

More was a devoted family man who lived in Chelsea, where Henry was a welcomed guest. He was renowned for his wit and wrote profusely. One of his books, *Utopia,* written in 1516, is still read and has been interpreted broadly both as a political manifesto and an essay on Catholicism.

Previous page:
Sir Thomas More portrayed whilst he was Henry's Lord Chancellor. A man of firm convictions, his reluctance to accede to the monarch's demands led to his ultimate fate. More's struggle with his conscience was dramatically explored in Robert Bolt's *A Man for all Seasons.*
The Royal Collection © 1994 Her Majesty The Queen

Opposite:
Cardinal Wolsey. This undated portrait, which is probably a copy of an earlier work, is appropriately on display at Hampton Court.
The Royal Collection © 1994 Her Majesty The Queen

Although a devout Catholic, More was interested in the new philosophies and religious doctrines of Erasmus, John Colet and Martin Luther. It was Erasmus who wrote a letter of introduction for Holbein to give to More on his arrival in England in 1526. When, after the fall of Wolsey in 1529, Henry promoted him to the post of Lord Chancellor, the divorce proceedings were well under way. More found Henry's attitude and actions deplorable, especially the rejection of Catholicism and the eventual break with Rome. His position became increasingly difficult as this highly moral man retained his devotion of Catholicism and was forced, in 1532, to resign for his beliefs and inability to accept the Act of Supremacy.

In 1534 More was arrested for treason, with John Fisher, and sent to the Tower where he stayed imprisoned for 15 months until his execution. On 1 July 1535 he was tried at Westminster, pleading that he was being accused under an Act of Parliament and not God's law. But he was a condemned man. Sir Thomas More was executed on Tower Hill on 6 July 1535; his head replaced that of Fisher, on the railings of Tower Bridge. His body was buried inside the Tower and his head in the Roper Vault at St Dunstan, Canterbury. The deaths of More and Fisher further infuriated European states.

In 1886 More and Fisher were beatified and canonised in 1935. Their feast day is 22 June and they are both recognised by the Roman Catholic Church, something unusual for English saints. Sir Thomas More, the martyr who died for his beliefs rather than accept the Act of a dictator, has been the source of endless essays,

biographies and analyses over the centuries. Throughout England there are schools and churches dedicated to the memory of More.

Thomas Wolsey 1475–1530

Thomas Wolsey was Henry's Lord Chancellor and political advisor for the early part of the reign. In 1511, as Dean of Lincoln, he became a member of the King's Council and Archbishop of York. He left York very much on its own, being busy with affairs in London. After the war with France he was made Bishop of Lincoln and Tournai. By 1515 he was Lord Chancellor, replacing Warham. Whilst Henry spent his days hunting, Wolsey ran the country, but all final decisions and policies were made by Henry. They were good friends, shared common ideals and together made a formidable partnership, plotting and scheming to make England a European power. Erasmus thought him as powerful as the king.

Not only was Wolsey very powerful, he was also rich and cultured. He founded Cardinal's College Ipswich and Cardinal's College Oxford, the latter on his demise was renamed King Henry VIII's College and is now Christ Church. Money for these foundations was gained by the early suppression of monasteries and religious houses.

Henry's divorce problems proved to be the cause of Wolsey's downfall and he was replaced by Sir Thomas More in 1529. He had been accused of treason for not agreeing to the divorce. In 1530 he travelled to Cawood, near York, but was arrested, on Henry's orders, by the Earl of Northumberland and began his journey to the Tower. However, he was by now very ill and the journey was slow. At Leicester Wolsey could proceed no further and died at the abbey on 29 November 1530, spared of his inevitable end at the Tower.

Thomas Wolsey was a great builder. Hampton Court and Cardinal's College Oxford were two of his achievements. He also built a 3.5-mile conduit from Kingston Hill and Coombe Hill to Hampton Court which went beneath Kingston and the Thames. The inspection points are still visible, although they are now on private property.

Opposite:
The palace at Hampton Court. The original buildings, dating from Cardinal Wolsey's ownership form a courtyard on the left. Under royal ownership, most notably during the reign of William and Mary when the architect Sir Christopher Wren designed additional wings, the building has been considerably expanded. The location of the palace on the Thames facilitated an easy journey to London in an age when river travel was by far the fastest form of transport.
Aerofilms

Above:
An entrance to a stairway at Christ Church showing the details of the Perpendicular style adopted.
Rickman's Gothic Architecture

Thomas Cromwell 1485-1540

Cromwell joined Henry's court in 1531, having been trained by Wolsey. Unlike other members, such as Wolsey and More, he was not a wealthy intellectual, academic or priest but a business man and solicitor. Cromwell was born in Putney and became MP for Taunton. His business acumen proved very useful to Henry during the valuation and suppression of the monasteries. Many Catholics thought him responsible for the anti-Papal feelings. In 1535 he was made Vicar General and Vicegerent, placing him above all the archbishops and bishops. However, even Cromwell fell out of favour and was executed on Henry's orders in 1540.

Leicester Abbey
Abbey Park Road
Leicester
Only the boundary walls and foundations of Leicester Abbey
remain, where Wolsey died and was buried.

Christ Church
Oxford
In 1523 Wolsey decided to establish a new college at Oxford University. By suppressing 22 monasteries and university buildings he was able to find the money and space for the new college. It took hundreds of workmen ten days to dig the foundations and at the end of a year Wolsey had spent £8,000 on the work. It was named Cardinal College after its founder but on Wolsey's demise, in 1539, Henry, wanting to be a respected patron and scholar, renamed it King Henry VIII's college. It later became Christ Church and is still a much respected college of Oxford University.

Christchurch Mansion
Christchurch Park
Ipswich
Suffolk IP1 3QH
01473 253246
1 Tue-Sun
2 No
3 Nearby
This historic house was formerly the Priory of the Holy and Undivided Trinity which Wolsey suppressed to fund Cardinal's College, Ipswich.

Above:
A second detail of the architecture at Christ Church. When Wolsey fell from favour, work on the part-completed college was suspended leaving the cloisters of the front quadrangle unroofed and the gateway — the famous Tom Tower — incomplete. The latter was completed almost 200 years later to the design of Sir Christopher Wren.
Rickman's Gothic Architecture

CATHERINE D'ARRAGON.

Mes parens, ma destinée, bien plutôt que mon choix,
Me firent tour à tour epouser les deux frères:
A mon second hymen les loix furent contraires.
Mais le cœur de Henri le fit plus que les loix.

vander Werff pinx.   Vermeulen sculp

CHAPTER 4:
HENRY'S WOMEN
AND CHILDREN

enry VIII's numerous marriages are legendary, even by modern day Hollywood standards. He also had several mistresses and illegitimate children. However, it is important to put Henry's marriages into their cultural and political contexts. Throughout Christendom the kings, queens and heads of states were constantly warring with each other or forming alliances against a common enemy and marriages between their eligible children were regarded as strategically necessary. A marriage treaty would be signed between states long before the children whom it concerned were of age and the treaty was nullified if the two nations became enemies. Catherine of Aragon's two marriages, firstly to Prince Arthur and then to Henry, as well as that between Henry and Anne of Cleves, were such political unions. Many European princesses were suggested as available to Henry after the death of Jane Seymour a few days after Edward's birth.

The necessity for families in the upper classes to have a male heir was enormous and there was great pressure on wives to produce a son. Women often had numerous miscarriages, and still-births, maternal and neo-natal deaths were common; pregnancy and childbirth were hazardous. Babies of the upper classes that did survive were sent to wet-nurses. They did not see their parents for months at a time and built a close relationship with the wet-nurse and her family. Sometimes the parents took a dislike to the nurse and then broke the bond by suddenly removing the baby and sending him or her elsewhere. The absence of the contraceptive effects of breast-feeding meant that non-breast-feeding, upper-class women were more likely to become pregnant than their wet-nurses, who might feed for years at a time.

Previous page:
Henry VIII married his first wife, Catherine of Aragon after the death of her husband, Henry's brother, Arthur. The Prince of Wales' wedding had been arranged between the English and Spanish crowns to cement an alliance and, after Arthur's death, a second treaty was signed. Henry and Catherine married in 1509.
The Fotomas Index

Right:
In order to get his marriage with Catherine annulled Henry resorted to the courts. This is a Victorian view of Catherine's trial.
The Fotomas Index

> **WIVES**
> DIVORCED, BEHEADED, DIED, DIVORCED, BEHEADED, SURVIVED...
>
> ## Henry VIII 1491–1547
> m. 1509 Catherine of Aragon (1485–1536) divorced 1533. Mary (Mary Tudor) 1516–58
> m. 1533 Anne Boleyn (1507–36) divorced and executed 1536. Elizabeth (I) 1533–1603
> m. 1536 Jane Seymour (1509–37) died 1537. Edward (VI) 1537–53
> m. 1540 Anne of Cleves (1515–57) divorced 1540
> m. 1540 Katherine Howard (1521–42) executed 1542
> m. 1543 Catherine Parr (1512–48) survived

Catherine of Aragon 1485–1536

In 1488 Henry VII and Ferdinand of Spain signed a treaty by which their children, Prince Arthur (Henry VII's heir) and Catherine of Aragon, would marry. When Catherine landed in Plymouth in 1501 with a huge entourage the couple had not met each other; they married at St Paul's Cathedral in London on 14 November. Months later, Prince Arthur died at Ludlow Castle, making Henry heir to the throne. The question of the consummation, or not, of this short marriage between two very young people was to be of vital importance years later. Both countries wanted to continue the alliance and Henry VII and Ferdinand signed a second treaty, this time for the future marriage of Prince Henry to Catherine. Initially Henry was uneasy, but eventually they married, a few weeks after Henry VII's death, in 1509. The Queen, Elizabeth of York, had died in 1503, devastated by her son Arthur's death.

The coronation of the newly married king and queen took place in Westminster Abbey on 11 June 1509. Letters written by them both at the time, to Ferdinand, convey their happiness and Catherine's well-being. This, the longest of all Henry's marriages, lasted 24 years.

Catherine was a popular queen and for many years accompanied Henry on his journeys, in great style and splendour. They both went to meet François at the Field of the Cloth of Gold in 1520, for example, and their joint coat of arms can still be seen on buildings.

However, the happiness of the marriage began to be marred by numerous miscarriages, some of them male babies, suffered by Catherine. Eventually though one child, a daughter Mary, born in 1516, survived.

Maybe because Catherine and Henry had married so young they began, after years of marriage, to grow apart and be bored by each other and in 1525 Henry had an affair with Mary Boleyn. After her marriage, he focused his attention on her sister Anne. Anne Boleyn is always perceived as lively and seductive, far more exciting than Catherine. By 1527 Henry was determined to marry Anne and the need to divorce Catherine became vital to him, though it was made more difficult by his wife's refusal to co-operate. Catherine's determination not to end her marriage and the Pope's continuous refusal to grant a divorce made Henry embark on a long course of destruction and change. This cost many lives, caused much debate and argument, split the clergy, isolated England from Europe and made way for the establishment of a Protestant church. Henry enlisted the courts to try and prove the marriage was not lawful. The Papal ambassador, Chapuys, remained loyal to Catherine and supported her in her fight against Henry. Lord Chancellor Wolsey's services were disposed of and Henry demanded his execution, but he died in Leicester before reaching the Tower. The new Lord Chancellor, Sir Thomas More, a devout and loyal Catholic, could not support the King when he proclaimed himself Head of the Church in England. More was beheaded in 1535.

In 1533 Cranmer, the new Archbishop of Canterbury, announced the marriage was unlawful and Henry immediately married the pregnant Anne Boleyn. The Pope meanwhile stated the marriage to Catherine was still valid and in Rome's eyes Henry now had two wives. The split was irretrievable.

Inevitably, relations between Spain and England became very strained. Catherine's nephew, Charles, and other European monarchs began to break alliances with England, isolating it still further. After the divorce Henry wanted Catherine and Mary to take the Oath of Allegiance and recognise him as the head of the Church in England; they refused and remained Catholic.

After the separation from Henry, Catherine lived at Ampthill and Buckden, finally moving to Kimbolton in Huntingdon in 1534. Mary was allowed no contact with her mother. To prevent Mary having any claim to the throne, Henry tried to declare her illegitimate, stating her parents' marriage had never been legal. He also demanded that Catherine revert to the title Dowager Princess of Wales, which she had been given in the period between Arthur's death and her remarriage. She refused, remaining Queen Catherine until her death on 7 January 1536, aged 50. She was buried in Peterborough Cathedral as wife of Arthur, Henry's brother, but not Queen. Chapuys and her supporters did not attend the funeral because her title of queen was not recognised at death; Henry chose to wear yellow and went to a party.

Anne Boleyn 1507–1536

The portrait of Anne Boleyn in the National Portrait Gallery is of a pretty, lively women with a humorous smirk on her face. Her father, Thomas Boleyn, had been one of Henry's envoys to the Netherlands in 1512. He was an ambitious man and keen to get Henry's attention. The family lived at Hever Castle in Kent. Henry conferred on Boleyn the title of Viscount Rochford in 1525 at the same time as taking Boleyn's elder daughter, Mary, as his mistress. However, Mary married, leaving her younger sister, Anne, to become the king's mistress in 1531. In 1533 she became pregnant. Henry, desperate for a son and heir, was determined the baby should be legitimate so they married secretly in January 1533. Some months later Cranmer announced the marriage between Henry and Catherine had been unlawful. Anne gave birth to Elizabeth in September 1533.

However, the people remained faithful to Catherine and did not approve of the divorce, nor the religious persecutions arising from the split with Rome. Anne, regarded by many as a seductress, was accused of adultery with various courtiers (including her brother, Lord Rochford), whilst Henry had taken an interest in Jane Seymour.

It is possible Anne had plotted to murder Henry in order to rule as regent for Elizabeth, but in any event Henry sent her to the Tower on 2 May 1536 with her brother and the other four accused men. Only one, Mark Smeaton, admitted he was guilty. Anne never denied or admitted guilt. All the men were executed on Tower Hill on 17 May. Henry, desperate to make Elizabeth illegitimate, divorced Anne before having her executed on Tower Green on 19 May. Meanwhile Henry dressed in white, had a party and set his mind on his future wife.

Jane Seymour 1509–1537

Henry first met Jane Seymour in 1535 when staying at her family home, Wolf Hall, in the Savernake Forest in Wiltshire. He was at the time married to Anne Boleyn although rumours of her adultery and ribald lifestyle were beginning to percolate. Eleven days after Henry ordered Anne's execution he married Jane, on 30 May 1536. She was to be the wife he loved most, producing the male heir, Edward, by Caesarean section and dying ten days later on 24 October 1537.

BOLEYN.

Henry was devastated by her death. The Holbein cartoon in the National Portrait Gallery shows half of the sketch for a painting, now destroyed, commissioned by Henry to include the most important people in his life. He stands huge and boldly to the left, behind is his father and in the other half, now lost, Jane Seymour, his mother and Edward appeared.

Anne of Cleves 1515–1557

Henry was 45 years old when Jane Seymour died and his health was already beginning to fail and the slim build diminishing due to his large appetite. On deciding to remarry various suitable European brides were suggested, including the widowed Duchess of Milan whom Holbein was despatched to paint for the king. However, Henry eventually chose Anne of Cleves, the sister of the Duke of Cleves from northern Germany, believing an alliance with a pro-Lutheran family would be advantageous in his stance against Rome.

Anne arrived in Dover from Düsseldorf in December 1539 with an entourage of 263 people. She and Henry met for the first time at Shooters Hill in January and, despite being repelled by her plain looks, he married her on 6 January. However, the marriage was never consummated and they divorced amicably the following June. For a period, after the demise of Katherine Howard, Anne believed that Henry might remarry her. She remained in England for the rest of her life.

Katherine Howard 1521–1542

Henry seems to have been oblivious of Katherine Howard's notoriety as a seductress before he married her on 28 July 1540, the day Thomas Cromwell was beheaded. She was Norfolk's niece and relationships with Culpepper and Dereham, two of her long-term lovers, continued during her marriage. Henry was now hardly the most agile of lovers, and his obesity and ulcerated leg made walking very difficult. The suppression of the monasteries was complete after four years of turmoil, pogroms and the uprising of the Pilgrimage of Grace.

In 1541 Henry and Katherine went on a trip to York, his only journey so far north. They stayed at Suffolk's (Charles Brandon) house, Grimsthorpe near Lincoln, and visited the Bishop's Palace. Culpepper accompanied them and continued his relationship with Katherine during the trip. Cranmer, aware of the Queen's adultery, informed Henry of it and on their return to London Katherine was imprisoned at Syon House. Culpepper and Dereham were executed for adultery, as was Katherine, in February 1542, at Tower Green.

ANNE OF CLEVES

DAUGHTER OF THE DUCK OF CLEVES   4ᵗʰ WIFE OF KING HENRY VIII

Married 1540.   Divorced 1540

Peut on s'imaginer une telle aventure ?
Mon portrait me fit reine et femme de Henry,
Mais mon original détruisant ma peinture
Je devins sœur de mon mari.

An authentic portrait engraved exclusively for the Court Magazine

VOL. XXI.   *N.º 101 of the series of ancient portraits*   1841

Court Magazine. N.º 5. Rathbone Place Oxford street.

Above opposite:
Although the bulk of Richmond Palace has disappeared, or is in Private grounds, the old gateway is still visible from the green.
The Book of the Tjhames

Opposite:
Jane Seymour, who married Henry shortly after the execution of Anne Boleyn, was probably the king's favourite wife and produced him with the much-desired son. Jane Seymour was, however, to die as a result of the birth.
The Fotomas Index

Left:
Following the death of Jane Seymour, Henry sought a further bride abroad. Eventually Anne of Cleves, sister of the pro-Lutheran Duke of Cleves, was selected. Henry was reputedly swayed by a complimentary portrait of her and was bitterly disappointed when he finally came face to face with her. The marriage was shortlived and the divorce was amicable.
Anne of Cleves House, Lewes

Catherine Parr 1512–1548

After the execution of Katherine Howard, Henry was, once more, without a queen and again various names were suggested to him. The Parr family, originally from Kendal, had been known to him throughout his reign. Sir Thomas, Catherine's father, was made a knight at the coronation but died in 1517. Catherine's first husband, Edward Borough, died in 1532 and, aged 21, she married Lord Latimer of Snape Castle. Latimer suffered during the mass uprising of the Pilgrimage of Grace, wanting to remain loyal to both the locals and the crown. He was taken hostage by Henry's troops but managed to survive, and died in 1543.

Henry began to pursue Catherine a few weeks before Latimer's death and married her on 15 July 1543. She was 31; Henry 52. Catherine was an experienced step-mother from both her previous marriages and had no children of her own. This was to be very important in the relationships she developed with Henry's three children, especially Elizabeth and Edward. The ailing Henry was not in need of a lover so much, but more the nurse and manager he found in Catherine. Through Cranmer she was introduced to Bishop Latimer. Although she was not a great intellectual she was one of the few Tudor women to write and have books published. Her Protestant leanings did, at times, concern Henry who by then was playing an odd game of alternately purging Catholics and Protestants, thus ensuring that nobody felt secure. In 1546 Henry almost sent Catherine to the Tower, believing she might have been contaminated by Anne Askew's illegal, Protestant writings. In fact, Anne Askew herself was executed.

When Henry died on 28 January 1547 it is thought Catherine was not with him. She did, however, attend his funeral and see him buried in St George's Chapel Windsor alongside Jane Seymour. After his death she married Thomas Seymour, Henry's former brother-in-law, and lived at Sudeley Castle in Gloucestershire.

Opposite:
Henry's last wife was Catherine Parr, whose Protestant beliefs almost led to her being imprisoned in the Tower. She was, however, to survive Henry.
The Fotomas Index

Left:
Owlpen Manor in Gloucestershire is one of many fine Tudor manor houses that can still be seen throughout England. The etching, by F. L. Griggs was produced in 1931 for the then owner of the house Norman Jewson.
F. L. Griggs, Courtesy Owlpen Manor

Kimbolton Castle
Kimbolton School
Kimbolton
Huntingdon PE18 OEA
1 Certain days in summer
2 Yes
3 Yes
Kimbolton was the last home of
Catherine of Aragon and it was here
that she died in the Queen's Room on 7
January 1536. All that remains of the
original Tudor manor house is the
basement area, most of the rest of the
house having been redesigned by
Vanbrugh.

Owlpen Manor
Owlpen
Near Uley
Gloucestershire GL11 5BZ
01453 860261
1 Apr–Sep
2 Yes
3 Yes
There is a portrait of Catherine of
Aragon in this fine example of an early
Tudor manor house.

Corsham Court
Corsham
Wiltshire SN13 OBY
01249 712214
1 Most of the year
2 Yes
3 Yes
The original manor belonged to
Elizabeth of York, Henry's mother, and
was given to Catherine of Aragon as
part of her dowry. On her death it
passed to Catherine Parr who kept it
until she died in 1548. The present
house is Elizabethan in origin.

Oxburgh Hall
Oxburgh
King's Lynn
Norfolk PE33 9PS
,01366 328258
1 Mar–Oct, most days
2 Yes
3 Yes

Henry appointed Sir Edmund Bedingfield to be Catherine of Aragon's steward and
comptroller of her household in 1533. He was present when she died at Kimbolton in 1536.
There is a letter on display from Henry VIII to Lady Bedingfield detailing Catherine's
funeral, including instructions about mourning cloth and the funeral procession.

Above:
The moated Oxburgh Hall in Norfolk. *AA Photo Library*

Inset:
A close-up illustrating some of the superb Tudor architectural detail to be seen at Oxburgh Hall.
AA Photo Library

Peterborough Cathedral
Minster Precincts
Peterborough PE1 1XS
01733 343342/897337
1 All year; visitor centre, Easter–Oct.
2 Donation
3 No
Catherine of Aragon was buried in the cathedral and in 1530 Cardinal Wolsey spent Holy Week and Easter here. It was the seventh wealthiest Benedictine abbey in England, with 37 monks, and at the dissolution the abbey church became the cathedral. There is a permanent exhibition about Catherine, Henry and the Benedictine abbey in the Visitor Centre. Catherine's tomb is in the cathedral, surrounded by Henry's banner.

Hever Castle
Hever
Edenbridge
Kent TN87 NG
01732 865224
1 Mar–Nov
2 Yes
3 Yes

Hever Castle was the home of the Boleyn family and there is still much evidence of their lives here. On the death of Sir Thomas Boleyn the castle was acquired by Henry, who gave it to Anne of Cleves in 1540. The Tudor rooms have been carefully restored and there is a portrait of Henry by Holbein and a tapestry bearing his coat of arms, as well as his bedroom with a huge four-poster bed. It was at Hever that Henry courted both Mary and Anne Boleyn. Anne's Bible, coat of arms as Queen, and a pathway in the garden dedicated to her are all here.

Opposite:
The west front of Peterborough Cathedral. This cathedral was to be the final resting place of Catherine of Aragon after she died at nearby Kimbolton.
AA Photo Library

Above:
Hever Castle was the family home of the Boleyn family and, appropriately, the castle's collection includes a portrait of Anne by an unknown artist after Holbein.
© *Hever Castle Ltd*

Left:
An aerial view of Hever Castle.
© *Hever Castle Ltd*

Penshurst Place

Penshurst
Tonbridge
Kent TN11 8DG
01892 870307
Henry stayed here whilst courting Anne (see page 149).

HM Tower of London

Tower Hill
London EC3 4AB
0171 709 0765
1 All year
2 Yes
3 No

Henry VIII used the Tower as a residence as well as a prison and execution site. As was the custom, he spent a few days here, in the Medieval Palace, immediately before his coronation. However, for two of his wives it was their final home; both Anne Boleyn (1536) and Katherine Howard (1542) were imprisoned and led to their executions on Tower Green, within the Tower Precinct. Other prisoners, like Sir Thomas More, spent months in the Tower before their executions outside the Precinct on Tower Hill, now Trinity Green. (See also the Royal Armouries page 102.)

The collection at Hever also includes portraits of (*Opposite*) Henry VIII and (*Left*) Mary Tudor, by Holbein and an unknown artist respectively.
© *Hever Castle Ltd*

Left:
The Tower of London served many purposes for Henry from Royal Palace to prison. It was in the Tower that two of his wives, Anne Boleyn and Katherine Howard, were to await their ultimate fate. Other notable occupants included Sir Thomas More who was executed for his unwillingness to accede to the King's divorce from Catherine of Aragon.
© *Historic Royal Palaces*

Following pages:
It was at Penshurst Place in Kent that Henry stayed while pursuing his courtship of Anne Boleyn.
© *Penshurst Place*

British Museum
Europe 15th–18th centuries, Gallery 46
There is, in the gallery, a Renaissance-style
clock which is thought to have been given to
Anne Boleyn by Henry. Lovers' knots surround
the engraved letters 'H' and 'A' (see page 20).

Penhow Castle
Near Newport
Gwent NP6 3AD
01633 400800
1 Limited times winter and summer
2 Yes
3 Yes
This was the first British home of Roger de St
Maur, a Norman knight, and his family who
were ancestors of Jane Seymour. The Seymours
moved to Wiltshire in the 14th century.
However, there is a miniature painting of Jane,
her seal and a document sealed by Edward VI
making the Earl of Worcester Steward of Wales.
The south façade of the house is as it appeared
when a Tudor manor house.

St George's Chapel
(see Windsor Castle page 157)
Jane Seymour was buried in St George's Chapel, as was Henry, next to her, years later.
The building of the chapel was begun by Edward IV in 1475 and finished by Henry VIII
in 1528.

Anne of Cleves House Museum
52 Southover High Street
Lewes
East Sussex BN7 1JA
01273 474610
1 Nov–Mar
limited, Apr–Oct
every day
2 Yes
3 Nearby
This Tudor house
formed part of
Lewes Priory, one
of the first
monasteries to be
dissolved by
Thomas
Cromwell. Henry
gave it to Anne of
Cleves as part of
their divorce
settlement. Inside
there are displays
about Anne.

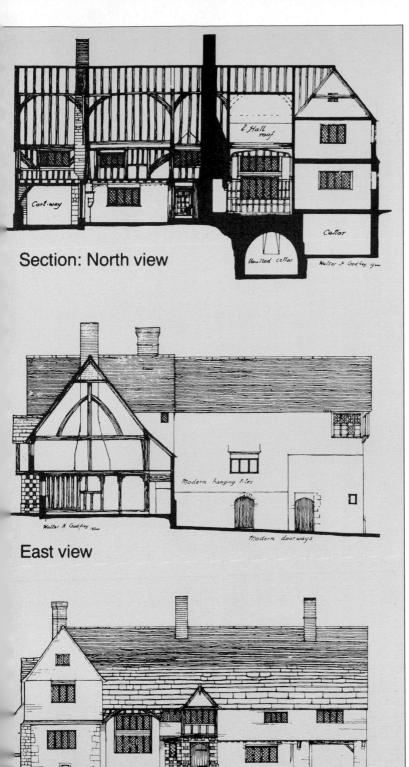

Section: North view

Cart-way

Hall roof

Cellar

Vaulted cellar

Walter H. Godfrey 1924

East view

Modern hanging tiles

Modern doorways

Walter H. Godfrey 1924

Walter H. Godfrey 1924

Sudeley Castle
Winchcombe
Cheltenham
Gloucestershire
01242 602308
1 Apr–Oct
2 Yes
3 Yes
After Henry's death
Catherine Parr
married Thomas
Seymour and lived at
Sudeley.

Children

Henry was cruel to his wives and his daughters. Mary, to her father's great annoyance, steadfastly refused to renounce her Catholicism or to sign the Oath of Allegiance. After the divorce from Catherine of Aragon, Henry declared Mary illegitimate on the grounds that her parents' marriage had never existed. His swift divorce from Anne Boleyn immediately before her execution ensured Elizabeth's illegitimacy. It was necessary to Henry that they should be illegitimate so they would have no claim to the throne. However, this need changed with the birth of Edward.

In her highly readable account of the six wives, Antonia Fraser writes of the good relationship Edward and Elizabeth had with Catherine Parr. She was the only wife able to give them any kind of mothering. Elizabeth, particularly, formed a very close friendship with her.

> **THE SUCCESSION**
> Edward
> Mary
> Elizabeth
> Between them Henry and his children ruled England for almost 100 years.

Opposite above:
After the death of Henry in 1547, Catherine Parr remarried and spent the remaining months of her life at Sudeley Castle in Gloucestershire.
AA Photo Library

Opposite left:
Edward VI in 1546; painted by an unknown artist, this portrait shows Edward at the age of nine, just prior to his father's death. Edward, the only child of Henry's marriage to Jane Seymour, was a sickly child.
The Trustees of Grimsthorpe and Drummond Castle Trust Ltd: photograph Courtauld Institute of Art

Opposite right:
Edward by an unknown English artist. Inheriting the crown whilst still a minor, Edward was to be under the guardianship of two Protectors during his short reign. The second of these, the Duke of Northumberland, attempted to organise a palace coup at Edward's death to ensure the Protestant succession. Lady Jane Grey was to be Edward's successor and she 'reigned' for nine days before Mary Tudor re-established the true succession. Lady Jane Grey, along with her co-conspirators, was subsequently executed.
From the collection of Dulwich Picture Gallery, London, on loan to Tredegar House.

Above:
An early portrait of Mary Tudor. Born to Henry's first wife, Catherine of Aragon, Mary grew up a staunch Catholic. In an attempt to stop her claim to the throne Henry had her declared illegitimate following his divorce from Catherine.
The Trustees of Grimsthorpe and Drummond Castle Trust Ltd: photograph Courtauld Institute of Art

Hatfield House
Hatfield
Hertfordshire AL9 5NQ
01707 262823
1 Mid Mar–mid Oct
2 Yes
3 Yes
Henry acquired a manor house, the old Palace, at Hatfield from the Bishop of Ely in 1538 and it became home to his children Edward, Elizabeth and Mary. It was under an oak tree there that Elizabeth heard she was Queen in 1558. There are portraits of Henry and his wives in the house, and the site of the oak tree can be found in the garden.

Framlingham Castle EH
Framlingham,
Suffolk, IP8 9BT
01728 724 189
1 Nov–March daily
2 Yes
3 Yes
Warned by sympathisers that the Duke of Northumberland was plotting to usurp her following the death of Edward VI in 1553, Mary fled to the castle at Framlingham (which was then held by the crown), where she gathered around her supporters in case she

needed to fight for her inheritance. It was at Framlingham that she was proclaimed queen. In the event the plot failed and England was spared a second civil war in less than a century.

Top:
Whilst Henry was alive Elizabeth, and the other royal children, lived at Hatfield House in Hertfordshire. It continued to be Elizabeth's house after Henry's death and it was here that she received the news of Mary's death in 1558.
© *Hatfield House*

Above right:
It was to the austere medieval castle at Framlingham in Suffolk that Mary fled to gather supporters when it appeared that the Duke of Northumberland was plotting to usurp her right to the throne. Mary succeeded to the throne in 1553. As part of her strategic policy she married Philip of Spain. However, the marriage — which was unpopular in the country, with people fearing Spanish domination — produced no children and the alliance with Spain was to achieve little for Mary's foreign policy. Calais, one of the few remaining English possessions in continental Europe, was lost to the French and when Mary died in 1558 the name of that port was said to be inscribed on her heart.
MHW/Peter Waller Collection

CHAPTER 5:
ENGLAND
AND EUROPE

Sixteenth-century Europe was made up of independent states or principalities. Marriage contracts united countries and family dynasties such as the Medici in Florence and the Hapsburgs in Northern Europe were major forces. The Tudors, in power since Henry VII's accession at the end of the War of the Roses in 1485, were Kings of England and France. For centuries the heads of states of what was called Christendom were answerable to the Pope in Rome and a common enemy, usually 'The Turk', in Constantinople, united them.

The formation of new alliances began to develop the concept of nationhood which, combined with the gradual growth of secularism, Luther's teachings in Germany and the Renaissance in Florence, as well as discoveries of new territories outside the continent, helped to define Europe as separate from Christendom. Suddenly questions were being asked about Christendom's own survival.

Unions developed between different states depending on the goals and whims of their monarchs. Henry VIII was very much part of these changes, regarding England as a European power and constantly vying with Spain or France. During his reign he went to Calais three times but only as far north as York once.

Relationships with France were usually tense; wars and skirmishes in the Channel were common. Usually, if Henry's troops were embroiled in a French offensive, the Scots would attack England along the northern border, with varying success.

Peace having been declared between England and France, Henry and François set about having a huge meeting in Val Dorée in 1520. Like many modern summits between heads of state, the main

Previous page:
Throughout his reign, Henry was conscious of the need to maintain alliances particularly once the conflict with the Catholic church developed. Treaties and weddings were arranged through the despatch of ambassadors and this shows an ambassador being received at Hampton Court.
The Fotomas Index

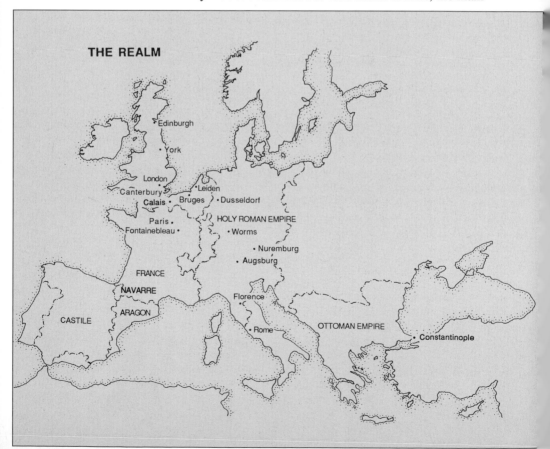

THE REALM

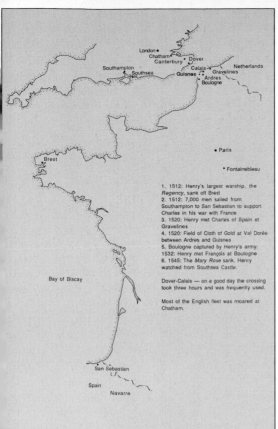

1. 1512: Henry's largest warship, the *Regency*, sank off Brest
2. 1512: 7,000 men sailed from Southampton to San Sebastian to support Charles in his war with France
3. 1520: Henry met Charles of Spain at Gravelines
4. 1520: Field of Cloth of Gold at Val Dorée between Ardres and Guisnes
5. Boulogne captured by Henry's army. 1532: Henry met François at Boulogne
6. 1545: The *Mary Rose* sank. Henry watched from Southsea Castle.

Dover-Calais — on a good day the crossing took three hours and was frequently used.

Most of the English fleet was moored at Chatham.

purpose of The Field of the Cloth of Gold was to display wealth and strength to each other. Henry and Catherine set sail from Dover to Calais in a fleet of 27 ships. They were accompanied by Lord Chancellor Wolsey, the Duke of Buckingham, and the Duke of Suffolk. Altogether the delegation consisted of:

(HENRY'S ENTOURAGE)
3,997 people
2,087 horses

(CATHERINE'S ENTOURAGE)
1,175 people
778 horses

A temporary palace was built in Val Dorée and the summit lasted for 17 days, ending with mass. The meeting was judged a success although Henry met Charles of Spain secretly afterwards to discuss a treaty. It was not long before England and France were at war with one another. In 1523 Henry unsuccessfully tried to capture Boulogne.

Catherine of Aragon as queen meant that, in the early part of the reign, relations between England and Spain were good. Gradually, however, her ill treatment from Henry, and the divorce, caused Spain to become an adversary. This was not only a period of great political and religious change but one of discovery, new inventions, artistic and intellectual developments, the impact of which is still apparent.

Only 16 years before Henry was born, William Caxton had printed the first book in English and set up the first press in England in 1477. Columbus, Magellan and Vasco da Gama were making their great voyages of discovery. New trading routes created great crossroads at towns like Nuremberg in central Germany. Spices were brought from the East and wool traded with the Netherlands. London was a busy port and home to merchants from all over Europe.

The great cultural Renaissance in Florence never influenced England in the way it did other northern European states. Although Leonardo da Vinci, Michelangelo and Machiavelli were all working in Italy during this period, it was Hans Holbein the Younger who came from Germany to be court painter. He was well aware of the Renaissance but became a portrait artist due to Henry's suppression of Catholicism and the creation of religious icons.

Of Henry's six wives, two — Catherine of Aragon and Anne of Cleves — were from European states. Henry arranged the marriage between his sister Mary, thereafter known as the French Queen, and Louis XII of France. Later he tried to enforce various marriage contracts between his two daughters and eligible European suitors, all of which were political marriages of convenience. Henry, due to his divorce from Catherine of Aragon, the Act of Supremacy, persistent snubbing of Papal authority, suppression of the monasteries and constant purging of Catholics had, by 1540, succeeded in isolating England from the rest of Europe.

Opposite:
Map of the major states of 16th century Europe.

Above:
Map of the major ports for the crossing from England to France in Henry VIII's day.

Above left:
The Field of the Cloth of Gold as portrayed in a painting from the Royal Collection at Hampton Court. Henry can be seen on horseback surrounded by Yeoman of the Guard. Also visible, in the extreme background, is Calais, which was then an English possession, and the castle of Hammes, which is surrounded by water. The painting shows the various temporary buildings erected on the site to greet Henry and Catherine.
The Royal Collection © Her Majesty The Queen

Left:
Although England's possessions in continental Europe had declined significantly during the previous century, Henry still claimed the French throne and a number of military expeditions were despatched from England. This engraving shows the departure of the English fleet from Dover in May 1520 *en route* to France for the meeting with François at the Field of the Cloth of Gold. Note the warships of the era; the *Mary Rose* would have looked similar when she was launched.
The Fotomas Index

THE DEPARTURE OF KING HENRY VIII. FROM CALAIS, JULY XXV. MDXLIV.

ENGRAVED FROM A COEVAL PAINTING, AT COWDRAY IN SUSSEX, THE SEAT OF LORD VISCOUNT MONTAGUE.

Above:
In 1544 Henry VIII attempted a further military campaign in France. At that time Calais remained an English possession and it was the departure point for Henry's army.
The Fotomas Index

CHAPTER 6:
ENGLAND AND SCOTLAND
ENGLAND AND WALES
AND IRELAND

The relationship between England and Scotland was tense throughout Henry's reign. For Henry the situation was compounded by Scotland's continuous alliance with France and the possibility, before Edward's birth, of the accession passing to Scotland. Border conflicts were frequent and bloody. Attacks, by the Scots, would often take place when Henry's forces were stretched to their limits in Europe. Tynedale, Resedale, Kelso, Jedburgh and Coldstream were often burnt and pillaged.

Henry's sister, Margaret, had married James IV of Scotland. He was killed at the Battle of Flodden in 1513, leaving Margaret as regent for James V, aged 17 months. Henry was concerned for their safety especially when, in 1515, James IV's cousin, the Duke of Albany, was sent from France by François to challenge them. He found them at Stirling Castle, where they surrendered, before going to Edinburgh. Henry later helped them escape to Harbottle Castle in Northumberland.

As there was still no male heir in England the problem of the accession passing to Scotland, via Margaret and James V, posed a great threat to Henry. Attempting to alleviate this and to form an alliance with France, Henry had agreed that his sister Mary should marry the elderly Louis XII in 1514. He died shortly afterwards and Mary, the French Queen, secretly married Charles Brandon. Eventually, the birth of Edward to Jane Seymour, in 1537, put an end to speculation about the accession. James V married Mary of Guise and their daughter, Mary (Queen of Scots) was born in 1542, six

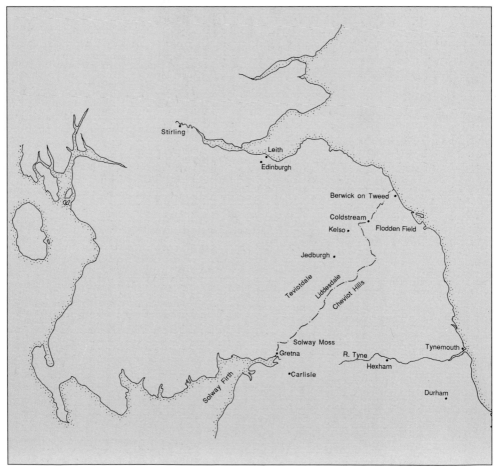

days before her father was killed at the Battle of Solway Moss.

In 1542, whilst François and Charles were declaring war on one another, raids again took place along the Scottish border. The English army invaded between Kelso and Jedburgh. Later Norfolk led the army, burning Eccles and Kelso, but the Scots outwitted the English. In November 18,000 Scots marched into England at Gretna for the Battle of Solway Moss where James V was killed. Henry immediately announced Scotland was his, demanding custody of Mary Queen of Scots and arranging her eventual marriage to Prince Edward.

Henry tried, unsuccessfully, to get the Scots to hand over Mary. There was a Scottish revolt at this which prompted Henry to instruct Suffolk to lead 8,000 men from Darlington to burn Edinburgh. This was planned for the following spring. During the winter of 1543 there were numerous skirmishes along the border near Teviotdale and Liddisdale. In April 1544 the English army left Tynemouth for Leith. They burnt Edinburgh in two days; only the castle survived. This did not quell the troubles and by 1545 there were 2,000 French soldiers in Scotland as a result of the war that Henry and Charles of Spain were waging against France. François wanted the return of Boulogne as part of a peace deal with England and Scotland. Henry refused.

As a separate country, Scotland had not been affected by Henry's policy towards the monasteries although the Reformation north of the border was to be even more fundamental in its effects later. However, the border warfare in the region was to lead to the destruction on several occasions of the major abbeys at Melrose, Jedburgh and Kelso. The destruction at Melrose was, for example, completed by the Duke of Somerset in 1547.

Above left:
Linlithgow Palace was the home of Margaret, Henry VIII's sister, when she married into the Stuart family. It was this marriage that led, ultimately, to James VI of Scotland, Margaret's great-grandson, succeeding as James I of England on the death of Elizabeth in 1603.
AA Photo Library

Border History Museum
Old Gaol
Near the Market Place
Hexham
Northumberland
01434 604011
1 Easter-October
2 Yes
3 Nearby
Like many of the towns on either side of the English-Scottish border, Hexham suffered much bloodshed, pillaging and fighting during Henry's reign. This small museum is in the first purpose-built gaol in England, built in 1330 and used until 1824. There are displays of helmets, pikes and spears; realistic sounds of screaming and charging horses as yet another home is plundered at night time; and a solitary prisoner stares up at you from the dungeon, waiting to die.

Royal Museum of Scotland
Queen Street
Edinburgh EH2 1JD
0131 225 7534
1 All year
2 No
3 No
The department of History and Applied Art at the museum has a joint exhibition, with the Scottish National Portrait Gallery, about the Stuart dynasty who ruled Scotland whilst Henry was on the throne in England.

Opposite top:
A detail from the battlements at Linlithgow Palace showing parts of the royal arms of England and Scotland.
AA Photo Library

Opposite below:
The Cistercian house at Melrose Abbey, situated in the Scottish borders, was founded by King David I with monks from Rievaulx in Yorkshire. It was one of the largest monasteries in Scotland, but never fully recovered after being sacked by the Duke of Somerset in 1547.
Peter Waller

Left:
Also founded by King David I in the 12th century, the Augustinian abbey at Jedburgh was to suffer severe damage from the invading English during the reign of Henry VIII before being finally suppressed in 1559. There are few more impressive sights than turning towards Jedburgh on the main A68 and seeing the red sandstone ruins dominating the view ahead.
Peter Waller

Edinburgh Castle
Edinburgh
0131 225 9846
1 All year
2 Yes
3 Not in summer

The great hall at Edinburgh Castle was built for the marriage celebration of Henry's sister, Margaret, to James IV in 1503. All subsequent Scottish kings and queens are descended from this union. When, in 1544, the Scots refused to allow the marriage between the infant Mary Queen of Scots and Edward, Henry sent in his army. There is a clear view from the castle of Leith, where Henry's invading army landed and then made their way to Edinburgh which they all but destroyed; only the castle remained intact.

Linlithgow Palace
Linlithgow
West Lothian
01506 842896
1 All year
2 Yes
3 Yes

Linlithgow Palace was the home of Henry's sister Margaret and James IV and there is evidence of the early Tudors in the design of part of the façade. James V was staying here when he went to battle, and lost his life, at Solway Moss in 1542, six days after his daughter, Mary, was born.

Berwick-upon-Tweed Borough Museum and Art Gallery
The Barracks
Berwick-upon-Tweed
Northumberland TD15 1DQ
01289 330933
1 All year, closed Mon in winter
2 Yes
3 Yes

The border town of Berwick has extensive Elizabethan fortifications and a Gun Tower from Henry's reign at Lord's Mount.

369. THE RAMPARTS AND PIER, BERWICK.

Left:
The border town of Berwick upon Tweed was regularly fought over by the English and Scottish, although by the end of the 16th century it was, politically, part of England. In an age when town fortifications were generally in decay, those at Berwick, were reconstructed during the reigns of Mary and Elizabeth.
Peter Waller Collection

Above opposite:
The Welsh counties created by Henry VIII in 1536.

England and Wales and Ireland

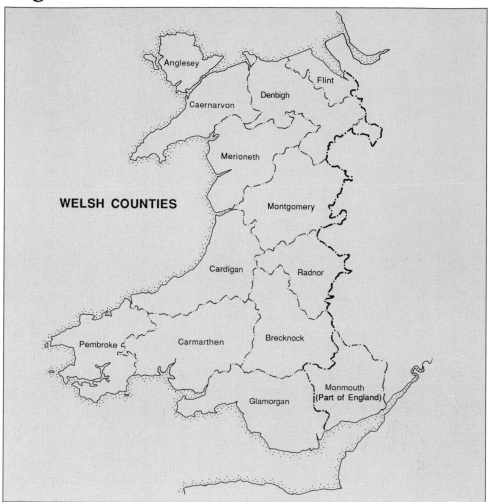

Anglesey

Flint

Denbigh

Caernarvon

Merioneth

WELSH COUNTIES

Montgomery

Cardigan

Radnor

Pembroke

Carmarthen

Brecknock

Monmouth
(Part of England)

Glamorgan

Wales

The relationship between England and Wales was very different from that with Scotland and there were never the border skirmishes and battles as those endured along England's northern border.

Henry's elder brother, Arthur, born in 1486, had been Prince of Wales and after Arthur's death in 1503 the title was passed on to Henry. The monarch's eldest son is still the Prince of Wales.

After divorcing Catherine of Aragon, Henry demanded she be called the Dowager Princess of Wales in recognition of her deceased first husband. Although she refused, wanting to be called Queen still, she was buried as the Dowager Princess of Wales, which caused upset amongst her loyal followers.

In 1536, at the beginning of his massive campaign to suppress the monasteries, Henry reorganised Wales by dividing it into counties and made Monmouth part of England. These remained until the 1974 boundary changes. The Welsh language and customs were suppressed, causing great difficulties as most people were unable to speak English.

Ireland

On his accession in 1509, Henry became King of England, France and Ireland. In 1535, an act was passed allowing England's domination of Ireland. After completing the suppression of the monasteries and the Act of Supremacy in 1541, Henry wanted more influence. There had been previous disturbances when he had tried to impose his will but this time, as in Wales, complete domination was the order of the day.

Below:
The dramatic lines of Edinburgh Castle dominate the skyline of the Scottish capital.
AA Photo Library

CHAPTER 7:
PAINTING, EMBROIDERY
AND ARCHITECTURE

enry's relationship with Rome had a profound effect on the development of English painting. During his reign, the Florentine Renaissance was at its peak and Leonardo da Vinci (1452-1519) and his fellow painters used the Bible as a source for their subject matter — the Annunciation, the Madonna and Child, the Crucifixion, the Last Supper. This, combined with their discoveries of perspective and new types of paint, became landmarks in the history of European painting. England, however, due to Henry, pursued a different path.

Centuries before Henry came to the throne, England, like other European countries, had witnessed the building of huge monasteries, abbeys and cathedrals in nearly every town which had provided scope for hosts of sculptors, carvers, stonemasons, guilders and painters. However, the monasteries were destroyed by Henry in his massive campaign of destruction (1536–1540) and with the suppression, any art form of a religious nature was banned. Had this not happened, English painting and embroidery might well have followed much more closely the style of the rest of Europe. Even in Protestant Holland, a balance was struck between painting everyday life, genre paintings, and Biblical stories. However, Henry would not allow this in England and the subsequent dominance of portrait painting as a genre was to last for generations, beginning with Holbein and continuing into the 18th century. A visit to the National Portrait Gallery confirms the strength and output of English portraiture from Tudor times up to the present.

Ecclesiastical embroidery had also been important; huge tapestries and smaller embroideries furnished monasteries, cathedrals and houses. They were not only decorative but provided invaluable insulation in the winter. Suddenly, however, their traditional subject matter was banned with the result that English embroidery came to be regarded as a luxury craft produced by wealthy women, a tradition it is only just beginning to extricate itself from.

Hans Holbein the Younger (1497-1543), who was born in Augsburg, Germany, became acquainted with the Renaissance through his friend, Albrecht Dürer, who had visited Florence and introduced the latest developments in painting, geometry and perspective into German painting.

Erasmus introduced Holbein to Sir Thomas More in 1526, and under his patronage Holbein produced an enormous collection of drawings of members of his family and people from the Court of Henry VIII (now in the Royal Library at Windsor Castle and not available for public viewing). These detailed drawings, in chalk and

Previous page:
A portrait of Anne of Cleves attributed to Holbein.
© *Hever Castle Ltd*

Above:
Charles Brandon, Duke of Suffolk, who rebuilt Grimsthorpe Castle for Henry's visit in 1541. This painting is from the school of Holbein.
The Trustees of Grimsthorpe and Drummond Castle Trust Ltd; photograph Courtauld Institute of Art

Opposite:
Although Henry was married to six wives, other women also drew his attention. Amongst these was Christina of Denmark, Duchess of Milan. In 1538, after the death of her husband and before her marriage to the Duc de Lorraine, she was painted by Holbein. The portrait was seen by Henry's ambassador, John Hutton, who was trying to obtain a portrait of Christina on behalf of the king.
© *National Portrait Gallery, London*

pencil, provide us with a visual record and insight into the characters of the time. Holbein was honest in his renderings; there are few beautiful people here. He had no inhibition about drawing what he saw both physically - spots, pimples, blemishes, warts, wrinkles, facial hair etc – and of the character within. For instance, popular history leads us to believe that Sir Thomas More was the pinnacle of goodness and fairness, the intellectual who was to die for his principles. Holbein's impression is of a man with tight lips and cold, scheming eyes. Renaissance influences are evident in his use of perspective and materials, and his ability to make his subjects lifelike, unlike earlier Tudor portraits.

By the time Henry noticed Holbein, the dissolution of the monasteries was well under way and his future as a painter of portraits established. He became very useful to Henry, painting portraits of women who might be suitable wives. His portrait of Christina of Denmark, Duchess of Milan, for example, was commissioned because she was under consideration as a suitable fifth wife for Henry. This simple, full-length oil painting, now hanging in the National Gallery, shows a sensitive, pretty young woman. Fortunately for her, by the time Henry saw the portrait he had other plans.

One of Holbein's more complicated paintings was commissioned by Henry whilst married to his last wife, Catherine Parr. Although the painting was later destroyed, one half of its cartoon now hangs in the National Portrait Gallery. As Henry was nearing the end of his life by this time, and was plagued by ill health, he wanted a painting of the people who had been closest to him in his life. In the cartoon we see a large, resplendent Henry standing to the left with his father, Henry VII behind him; to the right, we learn, stood Elizabeth of York (Henry's mother) and in front of her Jane Seymour with the infant Edward.

D KATH:DUCISSA
VIDUA ÆT: 25 N° D
DEINCEPS UXOR I
BERT

The National Gallery
Trafalgar Square
London WC2 5DN
0171 839 3321
1 All year
2 No
3 No
Holbein's full-length portrait of Christina of Denmark,
Duchess of Milan, hangs in the National Gallery.

The National Portrait Gallery
St Martin's Place
London WC2 OHE
0171 306 0055
1 All year
2 No
3 No
The Tudor Gallery contains an excellent collection of portraits of Henry VIII and
some of his wives and children. A portrait of the young Henry reveals him fiddling
with his fingers, making him seem very nervous, whilst later ones show him as a
huge, fat, self-confident king. Half of Holbein's cartoon for a painting of the people
he felt closest to dominates the collection. There are paintings of Henry's children
when young and of Elizabeth, resplendent as queen.

Tredegar House and Park
Newport
Gwent NP1 9YW
01633 815880
1 Apr-Oct Tue-Sat.
2 Yes
3 Yes
The Dulwich Picture Gallery in South London is renowned for its collection. It has
loaned a collection of early panel paintings of Henry and his family to Tredegar
House. The eight paintings are by unknown English artists and painted in oil on
wood.

Followers

There are numerous portraits of Henry and his court, painted by followers of
Holbein, in collections around the country. Some are copies of Holbein's original,
whilst others are the artist's own interpretation in the style of Holbein. The label on
such a painting should reveal its origin.

A Holbein follower closely copied the portrait of Henry in a wall painting at
Whitehall Place, which now hangs in the Walker Art Gallery,
Liverpool. Others hang in stately homes and small collections
throughout the country.

Holbein and the Court of Henry VIII by Jane Roberts, National
Galleries of Scotland 1993. This book contains reproductions of
some of Holbein's drawings of Henry and his court from the Royal
Library at Windsor. They belong to HM The Queen and, due to
their fragility, are rarely available for public viewing. Should they be
on exhibition, however, they are well worth seeing; Holbein was a
very honest portrait artist and did not feel obliged to make people
look beautiful.

Opposite:
Katherine Willoughby
de Eresby, Duchess of
Suffolk when Henry
visited, from the
school of Holbein.
*The Trustees of
Grimsthorpe and
Drummond Castle
Trust Ltd: photograph
Courtauld Institute of
Art*

Architecture

The reign of Henry VIII was to witness the final flowering of the Perpendicular style of architecture in England. Although the first traces of the Renaissance revival of classical architecture were starting to be seen — particularly in the details of major buildings and in the sculptures associated with monuments to the dead — the majority of major buildings, both those constructed by the monarch and the nobility as well as those ecclesiastical buildings built by the church before so much of its wealth was assumed by the crown in the late 1530s, continued the tradition of English Gothic architecture. Notable examples of this period of architecture can be found throughout the country and the following are amongst the most interesting and most readily accessible. It is important to note that the Tudor period was an interesting transitional stage in the development of architecture as a 'profession'. Although it is possible to trace individual craftsmen prior to the period, the concept of the named architect developed slowly during the course of the 16th century. Figures like Robert Smythson, who designed many of the grandest of Elizabethan country houses later in the century, did not exist until there was a pool of wealthy landowners willing and able to fund the construction of dramatic country houses. Two factors lay behind this change. Firstly, the dissolution of the monasteries released a vast amount of wealth to the laity and, secondly, those undertaking work had to be convinced that the state was secure. The 14th and 15th centuries had been marked by the continuing construction of domestic properties that were essentially fortified to a certain extent; the 16th century was to witness the development of country houses where ornament and comfort were the prerequisite rather than the need to exclude the unruly neighbours.

Westminster Abbey

Henry VII's chapel was begun in 1503 by the first Tudor monarch as a monument to his uncle, Henry VI. It was completed in 1512 and, with its superb vaulted ceiling and remarkable windows, the chapel represents a dramatic epitaph to English Gothic architecture. It is also worth noting that the very familiar west front at the Abbey is not quite what it seems and owes much to rebuilding in the 15th and 16th centuries. The west window and the lower parts of each of the towers were rebuilt in the late 15th century until work ceased shortly after 1500. The top part of each of the towers were completed in the early 18th century to the designs of Nicholas Hawksmoor.

Hampton Court

Henry inherited a substantial palace from Cardinal Wolsey. This had been built over a 10-year period from 1515 onwards and, on his final assumption of the property in 1529, Henry undertook much rebuilding to convert it into a royal palace. Amongst work undertaken was the construction of a great hall, which, with its Perpendicular tracery in the windows and open hearth, owed much to medieval traditions. Elsewhere at Hampton Court, however, some of the detailing, such as the carved medallions show that Renaissance thought was beginning to have an impact. It is unfortunate that the most grand example of Henry's architectural legacy, Nonsuch Palace, has all but vanished.

Opposite:
A Perpendicular window from St Michael Coslaney, Norwich, built during the reign of Henry VII.
Rickman's Gothic Architecture

Left:
The superb Perpendicular tower of St Mary's church, Taunton, in Somerset.
Rickman's Gothic Architecture

Above:
The wooden roof of the church at Trunch, Norfolk.
Rickman's Gothic Architecture

St James' Palace

This was originally a hospital for lepers, but was dissolved in 1532. Following this it passed to Henry VIII who proceeded to build a grand house on the site. Of this building, the most important survivals are the gatehouse on the northside and the Chapel Royal. Both date from the 1530s, although the decoration of the latter was redone during the 1830s.

Windsor Castle

St George's Chapel in Windsor Castle is one of the most splendid of all late Perpendicular buildings in Britain. It was started by Edward IV in 1475 and replaced an earlier chapel, established by Edward III to house the newly created Order of the Garter in 1348. The interior is dominated by the carved stalls that are allocated to individual members of the order with their banners above. The stalls date from the late 15th century. Also at Windsor is Henry VIII's gateway, which forms one of the main entrances to the castle. Although the castle itself dates back to the reign of William the Conqueror, much of the fabric was restored under George III, George IV and Victoria. The Gothic restoration of the early 19th century was designed by Sir Jeffry Wyatville.

Cleeve Abbey, Somerset

Just before the dissolution of the monasteries, Abbot William Sovell reconstructed the refectory of the abbey. The building, which survives, demonstrates that the church continued to undertake major work until the dissolution.

Christ Church College, Oxford

The college, founded by Cardinal Wolsey, was originally to have been called Cardinal College. When work started in 1525 it was intended that the quadrangle — the largest in Oxford — would have be cloistered and that the old Priory Church (the remains of which now form Oxford Cathedral) would be demolished once the new college chapel was completed. In the event, Wolsey's fall from favour in 1529 meant that the project was starved of funds and work was not completed. The famous Tom Tower was not completed until almost two centuries later when a design of Sir Christopher Wren was adopted. However, sufficient of Wolsey's grand vision survives to illustrate well the architectural style adopted. Of particular note is the stonework on the quadrangle walls delineating the intended vaulting for the cloisters.

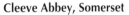

Above:
The west front at Bolton Priory showing the work unfinished at the time of its dissolution. The west window shows clearly the form of tracery which gave the Perpendicular style its name.
Ruined Abbeys of Britain

Bolton Priory, North Yorkshire

In 1520 the last Prior of Bolton, Richard Mone, started an ambitious programme to rebuild the west from of the church. However, the work was incomplete at the time of the Priory's dissolution in 1540 and the building today exhibits both the incomplete west front of the 16th century and the earlier west front of the 13th century that the new front was supposed to supplant. Bolton is also an example of a church where part — in Bolton's case the nave — has been retained as a church, leaving the remainder of the building as a ruin.

Fountains Abbey, North Yorkshire

Although there were undoubtedly rogues amongst the senior monastic clerics, there were also those of considerable learning and influence. One of these was Abbot Marmaduke Huby of Fountains Abbey. Huby, who died in 1526, bequeathed to the abbey the dramatic tower constructed over the north transept. He was also to rebuild the Abbot's Lodging at the abbey in a lavish style.

Lavenham, Suffolk

Vernacular architecture — ie that architecture that owed more to local tradition than imported ideas — flourished in the Tudor period and many of the country's best surviving half-timbered buildings date from the 16th century. One fine example is the Guildhall at Lavenham, in Suffolk, which dates from shortly after the foundation of the Guild of Corpus Christi in 1529.

Shrewsbury

The town of Shrewsbury, situated close to the Welsh border and the county town of Shropshire, can lay claim to possessing a number of superb half-timbered buildings in the charming centre of this historic market town. These include Ireland's Mansion (dating from 1575), the Abbot's House (on Butcher Row dating from c1450) and Rowley's House (which is now a museum). Prosperity came to the town once the border warfare with the Welsh came to an end. Parts of the old town walls survive. Other towns in Shropshire, such as Ludlow, also have attractive half-timbered buildings.

Bath Abbey

Refounded in 1495 on the site of an older abbey, Bath Abbey represents a superb example of late Perpendicular church architecture. Of particular note are the tracery and vaulted roof to be found in Prior Birch's Chantry. Chantries were chapels either attached to the main body of the church or built within, that were endowed for the saying of

Masses for the eternal soul of the person who had endowed it. Chantry chapels were amongst the most threatened of all the Roman Catholic features of churches once the Protestant Reformation took hold and many were destroyed by religious zealots.

Compton Wynyates, Warwickshire
This Tudor manor house was completed in 1515 by Sir William Compton, who was a friend of Henry VIII. The king, and many of his successors, stayed in the house on several occasions. The royal visits are marked by the royal monograms to be found decorating the plaster ceiling of the Henry VIII room.

Layer Marney, Essex
Built between 1520 and 1523 the gatehouse at Layer Marney, in Essex, is but a fraction of a much larger house that was planned but never completed. The building is interesting in that it demonstrates the transition from armed castle to more domestic buildings.

Rufford Old Hall, Lancashire
The Tudor great hall, dating from the late 15th and early 16th century, of this Lancashire manor is important in that it possesses some of the few surviving carved wooden screens that were used in traditional halls.

Opposite:
Shrewsbury, county town of Shropshire, can lay claim to many superb half-timbered houses dating from the 16th century. Amongst those accessible to the public is Rowleys House, which is now a museum.
Peter Waller

Above:
Rufford Old Hall is one of the finest preserved of all Tudor great halls. Completed in 1523 for its owner Thomas Hesketh, the hall possesses rare examples of Tudor wooden screens.
Peter Waller

Education

The 16th century was to witness a dramatic growth in the provision of education as a result of the wealth released by the dissolution of the monasteries. The number of King Edward VI Grammar Schools to be found throughout England is a mark of this as is the number of colleges either founded or re-established in the two university towns of Oxford and Cambridge. The following colleges were founded in the two universities between 1485 and 1558:

OXFORD
Brasenose 1509
Corpus Christi 1517
Christ Church 1546
St John's 1555

CAMBRIDGE
Jesus 1496
Christ's 1506
St John's 1511
Magdalene 1542
Trinity 1546

Part of each of these colleges' buildings dates from the date of foundation, although all have expanded considerably since they were first established.

Music

Royal patronage was an essential factor in the development of English music during the 16th century, just as the break with Rome was also to have a major impact. The period was dominated by a number of highly talented composers, whose work spanned both the liturgical and secular. Three were contemporaries — John Taverner (c1495-1545), Christopher Tye (c1500-73) and Thomas Tallis (c1505-85) — whilst William Byrd (c1542-1623) came from the next generation (although he and Tallis were jointly given the monopoly for printing music in 1575). With the inevitable confusion caused by the Reformation, life for composers, particularly of religious music, was not straightforward. However, despite straddling the period of Reformation, counter-Reformation and Elizabethan pragmatism, a remarkable corpus of works survive. Religious works in both Latin and increasingly in English predominate, but secular music was increasingly important. Private patronage was also important; John Taverner owed much to the favour of Cardinal Wolsey before the latter's fall from royal favour. The potential threats faced by composers and musicians in the period is illustrated by the fact that the contemporary John Merbecke (d1585) was condemned to death for heresy in 1544, although unlike other figures at the time he was to be reprieved.

CHAPTER 8:
THE ARMY
AND THE NAVY

E ngland's participation in European wars, the necessity to appear a major force, defence of the south coast from invasion and constant border troubles (especially with Scotland, and later suppression of the people) required a strong army and navy. These were important times as independent states emerged within Europe and replaced the loose federation of principalities dependent upon Papal authority. Inevitably, there was mistrust and power-broking between states in their quests for domination and authority. However, no matter how much these Christian states fought amongst themselves, they were united in opposition to a common enemy like 'The Turk' Barbarossa who ruled the Ottoman Empire which stretched across eastern Europe and north Africa. Conflicts with Soleiman and Barbarossa dominated events within Christendom, as armies pursued them rather than concentrating on inter-state skirmishes at home.

The Army

During Henry's reign men were conscripted into the army, especially if Henry was planning an attack and wanted to show his strength.

There were three wars with France in this period, and sometimes alliances with Spain, and throughout his reign the border with Scotland was always tense, battles and smaller skirmishes being regular occurrences. England's relationship with Scotland was further complicated by Scotland's alliance with France. This was useful for the Scots who often initiated a border raid when Henry's forces were dealing with the French, thus stretching his military power to the limits.

Sometimes mercenaries were hired, especially from the high Alpine Grisons region of Switzerland whose soldiers proved to be some of the fiercest and strongest fighters in Europe. Henry even employed Lutheran mercenaries from Denmark to show his allegiance was no longer with Rome.

The ravages into Europe and against Scotland were beset with problems: inclement weather, slow communication, mistrust and spying. Often assaults had to be delayed for the winter and it was not unknown for the army to mutiny due to hunger and lack of beer. Although two nations might have signed treaties of alliance they did not necessarily trust each other; envoys might be working for the other side and messengers mysteriously disappeared. Supporting the army was also very costly and, like all heads of state, Henry had to find the money from taxation. This led to problems at home, especially after a poor harvest or an overseas assault resulting in the closure of important trading routes. People became unruly at having to pay higher taxes for little evident benefit to themselves.

Soldiers, covered head to foot in metal armour, rode on horseback carrying long poles or pikes, about three metres in length.

Archery had been vital to warfare but, despite its precision, was declining. To be a skilled and accurate bowman took two-years' training. However, by the beginning of the 16th century the hand gun was being introduced, cutting down the training time and revolutionising weaponry and warfare with the use of explosives. Henry set up an armoury in Greenwich in 1515 which made suits for his men and horses.

Henry, the hunter, was also a soldier. If he did not send one of his professional soldiers to lead the army he went himself. In 1544 he went, against all advice from his advisers, to France. However, by this time his ill health and obesity meant that he was more of a liability than an asset to his men. In the Royal Armouries two suits of Henry's armour can be seen. One from his early years reveals his lithe, tall form but the second, from the end of his life, shows him with a fuller figure. His weight combined with that of the armour must have made work very difficult for the horse and the task of

Previous page:
Dover Castle.
*English Heritage
Photographic
Library/Skyscan
Balloon Photography*

Opposite:
From the painting by
W. H. Bishop *The
Warship Mary Rose
leaving Portsmouth
Harbour — Summer
1545*, showing in
detail how the ship
actually looked.
*Picture courtesy of the
Mary Rose Trust*

being an energetic soldier impossible.

As Henry's reign progressed and his authoritarian rule became more constricting the army was used increasingly to quell disturbances. In 1517 it was used to halt disturbances in the City of London between the indigenous population and foreign merchants. Henry and Wolsey sided with the foreigners because they needed their money, influence and trade. The locals felt they were paying high taxes for little reward and that the foreigners were profiting. After the Oath of Allegiance the army set on its own people, arresting and dealing with Papists, Lutherans, heretics, and anyone else who uttered a word against the king.

The Navy

The navy was vital to Henry's European campaigns, transporting men, horses, weaponry and supplies to France and Spain. Seven thousand men sailed from Southampton to San Sebastian in 1512 to support Charles in his war with France. In the same year the largest warship, the *Regency,* sank off Brest. Henry himself sailed from Dover to Calais in 1513 with a fleet of 300 ships, returning victorious.

The Fleet was also used for state occasions. In 1520, 27 ships ferried the King and Queen Catherine from Dover to Calais for the Field of the Cloth of Gold summit. Most of the Fleet was kept in the Medway and in 1547 a storehouse on Gillingham Water was leased to the navy. The mudbanks along the river enabled the ships to be beached and cleaned. The storehouse became, years later, Chatham Royal Dockyard, now the Historic Dockyard.

The most famous ship in Henry's fleet is the *Mary Rose* (originally launched from the dockyard in Woolwich in 1515 as the *Virgin Queen*) due to her recent excavation. She served the navy until 1545 when Henry dined on her in Portsmouth and learnt about a threat of invasion by the French. Shortly after he left the ship he watched, probably from Southsea Castle, as she sank. She was brought to the surface again over 400 years later.

Another great warship was the *Henri Grace à Dieu* (known as the *Great Harry*) which was built in Woolwich and fitted out at Erith. The *Great Harry* was the flagship of the Fleet (including the *Mary Rose),* leading it against the French in the war for Boulogne in 1545.

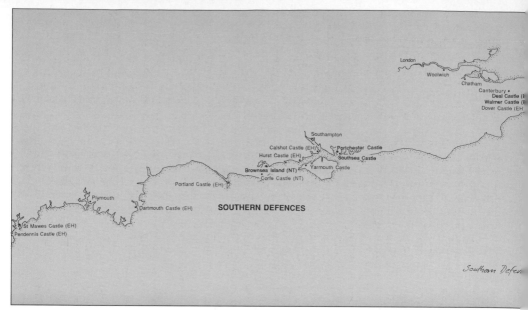

London
Woolwich
Chatham
Canterbury •
Deal Castle (E
Walmer Castle (E
Dover Castle (EH

Southampton
Calshot Castle (EH)
Hurst Castle (EH)
Portchester Castle
Southsea Castle
Yarmouth Castle
Brownsea Island (NT)
Portland Castle (EH)
Corfe Castle (NT)

Plymouth
Dartmouth Castle (EH)
SOUTHERN DEFENCES

St Mawes Castle (EH)
Pendennis Castle (EH)

Southern Defen

Postal Service

During medieval times each profession had its own post and these were well-established by the time that Henry became king. He appointed Sir Henry Tuke as the official 'Master of the King's Posts.' Sir Henry organised the posts making them very useful to Henry especially during the suppression of the monasteries and the Pilgrimage of Grace as well as laying the foundations of the modern postal service.

Southern Defences

Invasion along the south coast was, for centuries, England's greatest threat to security. Even during World War 2 the possibility of German invasion from France was very real. So, too, for Henry; he feared the French or Spanish might invade and there were frequent skirmishes in the Channel. France was, even then, only three hours away (Dover–Calais) on a good sailing day. In order to make the south coast secure Henry embarked on an extraordinary building project of forts and castles. These defences built by him from scratch, or incorporating existing strategic sites, extend from Kent to Cornwall and still stand. Henry designed many himself, often using a clover-leaf-like shape whose curved walls provided a maximum field of vision.

Deal Castle EH
Deal
Kent CT14 7BA
01304 372762
1 Apr–Oct every day, Nov–Mar Wed–Sun, Jan–Feb closed
2 Yes. EH members free
3 No
Deal Castle was designed and built by Henry. Anne of Cleves stayed here when she arrived in England in 1539 to marry Henry. Its strong bastions supported 119 guns. The austerity of life in the castle can be imagined by wandering through the dark passages into the basement and on to the battlements themselves.

Walmer Castle EH
Walmer
Kent CT14 7LJ
01304 364288
1 Apr–Oct every day; Nov, Dec, Mar Wed–Sun; Jan, Feb closed
2 Yes. EH members free
3 Yes
The castle was completed by Henry in 1540 but retains little of its original austerity. It is still the official residence of the Lords Warden of the Cinque Ports, an office held by Henry and today by HM Queen Elizabeth the Queen Mother. Outside, its solidity, defensive structure and strategic views over the Channel are reminders of its original purpose.

Dover Castle EH
Dover
Kent CT16 1HU
01304 201628
1 All year
2 Yes. EH members free
3 Yes
There has been a castle here since 1216. Although Henry did not build it, he often stayed here before sailing to France.

Opposite above:
Map showing the defences along the south coast during Henry VIII's reign.

Opposite below:
Deal Castle from the air showing clearly the design of the coastal forts built during the reign of Henry VIII. Experience had shown that a circle was a more secure shape for defensive structures — lacking the angles that could easily be undermined and not providing a flat surface so that incoming canon balls tended to be deflected — whilst the use of interlinked circles meant that the 119 canon based at the site could be used for crossfire and thus improve the castle's defensive qualities.
English Heritage Photographic Library/Skyscan Balloon Photography

Southsea Castle
Clarence Esplanade
Southsea
Hampshire PO5 3PA
01705 827261
1 Apr-Oct every day; Nov-Mar weekends only
2 Yes
3 Nearby
It is thought that Henry designed Southsea as part of the defence of the Solent in 1544.
He and his army were encamped around it in 1545 and it was probably here that he
watched the *Mary Rose* sink. Inside the castle are various artefacts discovered on the
Mary Rose, and exhibits showing the Tudor fortifications of Portsmouth.

Portchester Castle EH
Castle Street
Portchester
Hampshire PO16 9QW
01705 378291
1 All year
2 Yes. EH members free
3 Yes
The castle had been built long before Henry came to the throne and had been strategic for previous monarchs. Henry made Viscount Lisle its Vice Admiral in 1525 and Henry visited in 1527 when a new store house for his ordnance was built. Portchester was considered of little importance in Henry's defensive building campaign.

Calshot Castle EH
Calshot Spit
Fawley
Hampshire SO4 1BR
01703 892023
1 Apr–Sep every day
2 Yes. EH members free
3 Yes
Calshot was built by Henry in 1539 and is of a completely circular design. Although it has been changed much since the 16th century, the views from the top give a good indication of its strategic importance.

Hurst Castle EH
Keyhaven
Near New Milton, Lymington
Hampshire
01590 642344
1 Apr–Oct every day; Nov–Mar weekends only
2 Yes. EH members free
3 At Keyhaven ferry
Located on a pebble spit south of Keyhaven; take the ferry from Keyhaven or walk along the spit.

This was Henry's pride and joy and was regarded as his most sophisticated design, though the Victorians added two long, low 'wings' to Henry's original. The castle's position combined with powerful currents in the Solent meant that enemy ships stood little chance of coming ashore.

Opposite:
Portchester's origins date back to the Roman era and it remained an important strategic site until Henry's reign. Although he visited the castle, little was done to modernise it. Compare the layout of this more traditional castle design, its keep and massive walls, with the more compact designs that emerged during Henry's reign.
English Heritage Photographic Library/Skyscan Balloon Photography

Above:
A view of Calshot Castle from the south.
English Heritage Photographic Library

Below:
A mid-18th century engraving of Hurst Castle by Buck. The illustration shows the Isle of Wight in the background along with the Needles. The castle is flying the Union Flag. Note that the flag includes only the crosses of St George and St Andrew; the inclusion of the Irish cross of St Patrick occurred only after the Act of Union in 1801.
English Heritage Photographic Library

THE EAST VIEW OF HURS...

This Castle was built by K. H. VIII. for the Defence of th... Neck of Land shooting out beyond the main Land of Hamps... Yarmouth in the Isle of Wight, where the Sea is not abov...

1 The Isle of Wight.
2 The Needles.

el or Paſage call'd the *Needles*. It is on a narrow
...anding the Sea every way: And is alſo over against
...iles over.

J & N Buck delin et ſculp. 1733.

Above:
Yarmouth Castle.
English Heritage Photographic Library/Skyscan Balloon Photography

Opposite:
The ruins of Corfe Castle dominate the south Dorset countryside.
AA Photo Library

Yarmouth Castle EH
Yarmouth
Isle of Wight PO41 0PB
01983 760678
1 Apr–Oct every day
2 Yes. EH members free
3 No
This, Henry's last link in the defensive chain, was square rather than circular like his other designs. Two of the four sides stand on the sea edge and the other two were surrounded by a moat, making it impenetrable.

Brownsea Island NT
Poole Harbour
Dorset
01202 707744
1 Apr–mid Oct every day
2 Yes. NT members free
3 At Sandbanks
Although there is no evidence of Henry on Brownsea Island it was, with nearby Corfe Castle, part of the south's traditional defences.

Corfe Castle NT
The Square
Corfe Castle
Wareham
Dorset BH20 5EZ
01929 481294
1 Feb–Oct every day, Nov–Feb, weekends only
2 Yes, NT members free
3 Nearby
The ruins of Corfe Castle stand dramatically defending a gap in the Purbeck Hills around Wareham and Poole. It was neither built nor destroyed by Henry but from the top you can see exactly why it was important for the defence of the hinterland. In the distance the waters of Poole Harbour are clearly visible and any approaching invader would be dealt with long before they reached Corfe.

Portland Castle EH
Portland Harbour
Weymouth
Dorset DT5 1AZ
01305 820539
1 Apr–Oct every day
2 Yes. EH members free
3 Yes
Portland is the best preserved of Henry's castles
and is still fascinating to explore, inside and out. Its
curved front gives excellent viewing positions.

Dartmouth Castle EH
Dartmouth
Devon TQ6 0JN
01803 833588
1 Easter–Sep every day; Oct–Easter Tue–Sun.
2 Yes. EH members free
3 Yes
Building of the castle, to defend the Dart estuary,
began in 1481 and Henry added to the fortifications.

St Mawes Castle EH
St Mawes
Falmouth
Cornwall TR2 3AA
01326 270526
1 Apr–Oct every day; Nov–Mar Wed–Sun.
2 Yes. EH members free
3 Yes
Gun ports focus on every possible point of attack in
this clover-leaf shaped bastion built by Henry. It is
an excellent example of this type of design and
there are still good viewing positions. The castle
was built in conjunction with Pendennis across the
Fal estuary to protect safe anchorage in the
Channel.

Pendennis Castle EH
Pendennis Head
Falmouth
Cornwall TR11 4 LP
01326 316594
1 All year
2 Yes. EH members free
3 Nearby
Henry built Pendennis in conjunction with St
Mawes across the estuary and
it is the most westerly of the
defences. Its circular shape
makes it quite forbidding and
inside there are endless
interlocking rooms to explore,
as well as a re-enactment of a
Tudor battle.

Right:
The keep of
Pendennis Castle
viewed from the
south.
*English Heritage
Photographic
Library*

The *Mary Rose* Exhibition
Portsmouth Naval Heritage Trust
College Road
HM Naval Base
Portsmouth PO1 3LX
Hampshire
01705 839766
1 All year
2 Yes
3 Nearby
In July 1545 Henry VIII dined on
the *Mary Rose;* shortly after

disembarking he watched her sink, probably from Southsea Castle. The *Mary Rose* and
the remains of the 700 men on board lay on the sea bed for over 400 years. In 1982 she
made history again as the world's longest archaeological exploration. Her restoration is
on going and the latest process in this long procedure can be witnessed. Hoards of
combs, purses, silk, leather jerkins, herbs, ointments and surgeons' tools survived the
underwater ordeal and are on exhibition.

Right:
Henry's navy was normally based at Chatham on the Medway in Kent. Until its closure in the early 1980s, Chatham remained an important naval base and a significant number of historic buildings dating from the 17th century onwards survive. There is also a display describing how a wooden warship was constructed. The foreshore, where Henry's fleet would have been maintained, has long since disappeared through the construction of dry-docks and covered working areas — as illustrated — but there is much at the historic dockyard that recalls graphically the navy in the age of sail.
Peter Waller

The Historic Dockyard, Chatham
Chatham
Kent ME4 4TE
01634 812551
1 Easter–Oct every day, Nov–Feb Wed, Sat, Sun
2 Yes
3 Yes
Henry kept most of the Fleet in the Medway, the
mudbanks enabling the ships to be beached and
cleaned easily. In 1547 a storehouse on Gillingham
Water was rented to him; this was to be the beginning of
the development of Chatham Royal Dockyard until it
closed in the 1980s. It is now a museum about the
history of the dockyard and there are some 16th-century
guns in the Ordnance Gallery.

Erith Museum
Erith Library
Walnut Tree Road
Erith
Kent DA8 1RS
01322 526574
1 Afternoons Mon, Wed, Sat all year
2 No
3 Yes
The flagship of Henry's Fleet, *Henri Grace à Dieu,*
known as the *Great Harry,* was built in Woolwich and
fitted in Erith in 1514. A model of this warship and an
account of her fitting out are on display at the museum.

The Royal Armouries
HM Tower of London
Tower Hill
London EC3 4AB
0171 709 0765
1 All year
2 Yes
3 No
It is at the Royal Armouries that one can best gauge
Henry's size, both as a young athlete and an older,
immobile army leader. Two suits show the difference.
The smaller suit was worn by Henry at the Field of the
Cloth of Gold whilst the bigger one had to encompass
his 56in-waist measurement making the combined
weight of him and the armour quite a task for his horse.
The history of arms and armour is covered describing
their uses for hunting and sport, self defence and in
warfare. There is a display about the infantry in Henry's
time with examples of longbows, muskets, swords,
daggers and armour. Other exhibits include a Grotesque
Helmet given to Henry by Maximilian I in 1514;
lances belonging to the Duke of Suffolk, Charles
Brandon; field and tournament armour; and
Henry's arsenal of gun shields, pikes and javelins.
(See also pages 24, 45 and 147.)

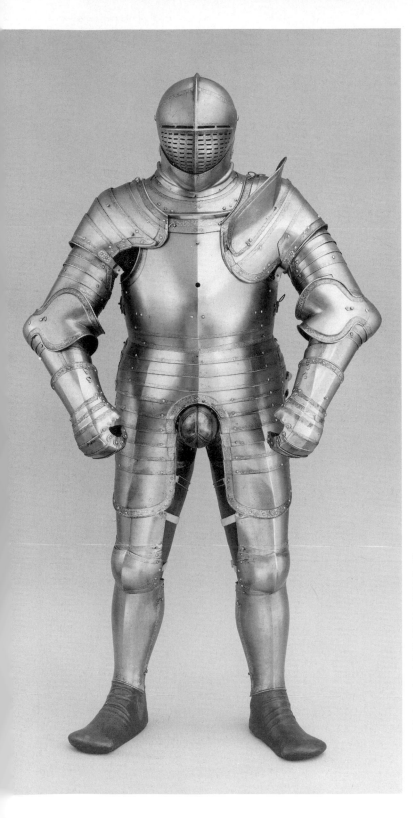

Opposite:
Foot combat armour
intended for use by
Henry VIII at the
Field of Cloth of Gold
in 1520 whilst he was
still a slim young man.
© *The Board of
Trustees of the Royal
Armouries*

Left:
Armour assembled for
the Foot Combat in
1540 for the older and
fatter Henry.
© *The Board of
Trustees of the Royal
Armouries*

Art Gallery and Museum

Kelvingrove
Glasgow G3 8AG
0141 357 3929
1 All year
2 Free
3 Yes

Amongst the collection of arms and armour here there is a crossbow probably made for Henry in 1527 and Greenwich armour made for the Earl of Pembroke and his horse in 1550. The Earl married Catherine Parr's sister. There are also other examples of armour from Henry's armoury at Greenwich.

Godolphin House

Breage
Helston
Cornwall TR13 9RE
01736 762579
1 May–Sep
2 Yes
3 Yes

William Godolphin was knighted by Henry in 1544 for his assistance in the seige of Boulogne. At Henry's request he had supplied 50 Cornish miners to assist in the seige and others who were expert at blowing tin. The oldest part of the house is of Tudor origin; the dining room survives from the period along with furniture, state papers and portraits.

Top:
Not all armour was as sophisticated as that provided for the King and for the leading nobles; this mid-16th century cabasset, or helmet, would have been worn by the foot soldiers of Henry's reign. This example is part of the armoury at Godolphin House.
Godolphin House.

Above right:
The Achievement of Arms presented to William Godolphin by Henry VIII for his valour at the siege of Boulogne in 1544. This now hangs in the dining room at Godolphin House.
Godolphin House

Right:
The dining room at Godolphin House is a survival from the 16th century and its displays include Tudor paintings and furniture.
AA Photo Library

THE
Historie of the
REFORMATION
of the
CHURCH of ENGLAND

SUPERSTITION

RELIGION

THE HOLY BIBLE

THE POPES SUPREMACY

PIPES DECREES

LONDON
Printed for Ric: Chiswell

R. White Sculpsit

CHAPTER 9:
ROME AND THE ACT
OF SUPREMACY

B y 1534 Henry's personal determination to end his marriage, combined with Catherine of Aragon's unwillingness to co-operate in the procedures, resulted in some of the greatest upheavals in English history. Until then England was a Catholic country and the Pope, in Rome, was head of the church throughout Christendom; both monarchs and clergy were answerable to him.

England was not the only country undergoing a cultural revolution. The Renaissance was well established in Florence; Vasco da Gama, Magellan, Columbus and others were making their great voyages of discovery; Erasmus and Luther publicised their thoughts about Papal authority and the new Protestantism. Christendom was undergoing great changes, secular movements were being embraced and a new group of European states was to evolve. However, it was only in England that the changes in the relationship with Rome were being pursued for such personal reasons.

In 1517 Luther nailed his 95 theses to a church door in Wittenberg, Germany. Desperate to unite Christendom against any threat from 'The Turk', the Pope regarded this as heresy. On a visit to Calais in 1520, Henry met Erasmus who tried, unsuccessfully, to persuade him to demand that the Pope stop his anti-Lutheran activities. In response to these demands Henry wrote the *Assertion of the Seven Sacraments,* opposing Luther. The Pope, delighted with Henry's attack, made him and his successors 'Defender of the Faith.' The letters FD still appear on coins, in recognition of this title. Thirteen years later, after many deaths and persecution, Henry proclaimed himself Head of the Church in England.

As relationships with Rome became increasingly strained Henry began to contemplate Luther's teachings. However, for the devout Catholic, Sir Thomas More, they would always be heretical, leading him to write his *Answer to Luther* in 1523.

By 1527 Henry had fallen in love with Anne Boleyn and the following year his divorce proceedings were made public. Wolsey, although he opposed the divorce, was no longer popular; people regarded him responsible for increased taxes. In May 1529 the divorce issue had reached the courts and Wolsey's term as Lord Chancellor ended a few weeks later. By November, Sir Thomas More was Lord Chancellor. Henry, although still officially married to Catherine, had made his affair with Anne Boleyn public.

The Pope disapproved of Henry's divorce and his interest in Luther. Henry, meanwhile purged heretics, Lutherans and Papists in turn. European heads of state increasingly moved away from England, appalled at his treatment of Catherine and his defiance of the Pope. Charles of Spain, Catherine's nephew, supported Rome whilst François and Henry tried to side against him, thus altering former allegiances.

By 1532 Sir Thomas More found his position untenable and resigned as Lord

à CLEM. VII. PONT. ROM. salutatus: HEROS laudatus, et Princeps bonus, erga bon̄ integras sine affectus, quorum Princeps ERASMVM ROT. Colit et amavit. EDVARDVM V Marium et Elisabetham, ex f. prognatæ Regni Angliæ ex ordine reliquit: Cæterum Io. Fissherū Episc Roffen. Thomā Mori Cancellariū regni aliorumq̃ supplicijs: Virtutes suæ famam paulo immin̄ut Con regnalⁱⁿ XXXVIII. ann. cœpit ætatis ānō LVII, à reparatā Saluti: ꝯ. D. XLVI.

106

Chancellor. He was later sent to the Tower with Archbishop Fisher who was made a Papal Cardinal in 1534; both were executed for treason in 1535.

Things came to a head when Anne Boleyn announced she was pregnant. Henry, anxious for a legitimate male heir, was determined to marry her before the baby's birth. So, secretly, in 1533 they married. This caused the final split with Rome where he was still regarded as married to Catherine. Henry, to emphasise the break, announced that he was the ruler in England with no-one standing between him and God. He became the first English monarch to be called 'Your Majesty'.

Meanwhile, Cranmer had become Archbishop of Canterbury and in May 1533 he announced that the marriage between Catherine and Henry had been unlawful, thus allowing them to remarry. Unleashed from Papal authority, Parliament passed an act in 1534 confirming Henry as supreme Head of the Church in England. Clergy and other officials had to swear an Oath of Allegiance to the King, Queen and their children and not to God. Henry demanded that any references to the Pope should be deleted from all prayer books. It was treason to deny Henry's authority and supremacy; thousands of people were arrested and executed as a result.

Henry's self-declared supremacy gave him even more confidence to push through the reforms he wanted, no matter how much hardship and terror he caused. Purging of heretics, Anabaptists, Papists and Lutherans were all undertaken by Henry's forces. He operated in such a way that no-one knew where they stood.

Above:
A piece of Tudor propaganda showing Henry seated on the throne with, to his right, his advisers Thomas Cromwell and Thomas Cranmer. At Henry's feet lies the prostrate figure of Pope Clement, emphasising the King's power over the Catholic church.
The Fotomas Index

107

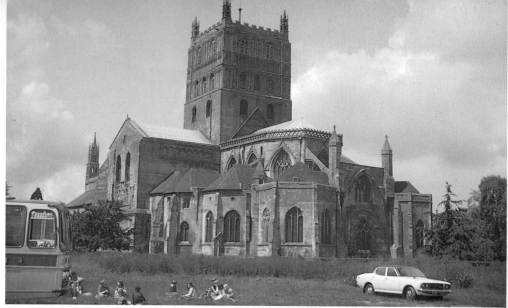

Above:
Amongst the grandest of all the monasteries acquired by the local population from Henry's Commissioners is that at Tewkesbury which was acquired by the town for the sum of £400.
MHW/Peter Waller Collection

Right:
The organisation of the church in England remained largely unchanged with the Archbishop of York continuing as the Primate of England and the Archbishop of Canterbury as the Primate of All England. The pre-Reformation sees also survived with three additions — Chester and Peterborough in 1541, and Bristol in 1542; the cathedral of the former is illustrated here. This structure of the church remained until growth of industrial cities of the north led to the creation of further bishoprics.

The Church of England

The split with Rome, caused by Henry VIII's need to divorce Catherine of Aragon, altered the course of Catholicism in England and prepared the way for the establishment of a Protestant Church of England. The monarch is still the Head of the Church, a claim first made by Henry.

Your Majesty

After proclaiming himself Head of the Church in England, Henry was called 'Your Majesty', still the correct title for the monarch.

The Bible in English

Throughout the pre-Reformation church, religious services were undertaken in Latin — the language of the learned rather than the masses, even if by 1500 much of the Latin used had become debased. Increasingly, reformers within the church came to the continued use of Latin as a barrier to the fuller understanding of the church's message amongst the uneducated and the 15th and 16th centuries were to witness the publication of non-Latin versions of the Bible in many European countries.

In 1494 William Tyndale was born in Gloucestershire. Becoming a priest, he was to become one of the most influential clerics of his age. Forced to flee abroad, Tyndale was to translate the Bible from Greek and Hebrew into English, which were printed on the continent. Vernacular translations of the Bible were seen as part of heretical actions of the Reformers and, as a result of his actions, Tyndale became a wanted man. Eventually captured by agents acting on behalf of Henry VIII in Brussels, he was imprisoned for 16 months before being condemned to death for heresy. He was executed on 6 October 1536 when he was strangled before being burnt at the stake. In April 1994 the British Museum acquired the only surviving complete copy of the first edition. It now forms part of the Museum's collection, along with other items associated with the English Reformation, such as Anne Boleyn's personal copy of the 1534 translation of the New Testament.

The Tyndale translation of the Bible was to form the basis of the Authorised edition of King James I in 1611 and is thus the source of many well-known phrases, such as 'fight the good fight.' The opening lines of the Gospel of Saint John are amongst the most familiar of all Christian writing:

'In the beginning was that word and that word was with God and God was that word. The same was in the beginning with God. All things were made by it and without it was made nothing that made was. In it was life and life was the light of me and the light beneath in darkness and darkness comprehended it not.'

Left:
Although the dissolution of the monasteries led to the destruction of numerous churches throughout England and Wales, in a number of places the old abbey church was retained, often through the efforts of the local population, as a parish church. Notable examples of this include Shrewsbury Abbey, Tewkesbury Abbey and, as illustrated here, Howden Minster in Yorkshire. Although the church may have survived in whole or in part, the monastic buildings were often demolished leaving part of the building as a ruin.
Peter Waller

British Museum
Great Russell Street
London WC1 3DG
0171 580 1788
1 All year
2 No
3 No
There are various letters in the King's Library, including one written by John Fisher to Thomas Cromwell in 1534 indicating his refusal to accept Henry as head of the Church. Thomas Cromwell's notes remind him to write to Mary demanding she accept the title 'Princess Dowager'. The Department of Coins and Medals has numerous pieces from this period.

The Museum
Public Record Office
Chancery Lane
London WC2 1LR
0181 876 3444
1 All year
2 No
3 No
The museum has various documents and bulls relating to Henry. Perhaps the most important is the Golden Bull, a coin and manuscript, bestowed on Henry as Defender of the Faith by Pope Leo X in 1521 in recognition of his attack on Luther. All coinage since bear the letters 'FD' in recognition of the monarch's position. There is a Papal Grant of Privileges to Cardinal College Oxford which was founded by Wolsey and is now Christ Church. Various documents sanction the suppression of Papal authority in Tonbridge and demands for the resources to be placed in Cardinal College.

Execution Sites
In London there were execution sites at Tyburn (Marble Arch), Smithfield, Tower Hill (now Trinity Green, outside the Lloyds of London, former Port of London Authority building) and on Tower Green in the precinct of the Tower. Executions took different forms depending on the crime and the accused's relationship with Henry. Not even his closest friends or wives were spared from this fate, should he demand it.

Catharine of Aragon.

Jane Seymour.

Anna Boleyne.

CHAPTER 10:
THE MONASTERIES
1536-1540

Between 1100 and 1500 northern Europe witnessed an unprecedented building programme of cathedrals, monasteries and churches. These Catholic institutions still stand, well-maintained, in France, Germany, Holland and Belgium, and many still practise the religion for which they were originally built.

In England, though, the story is very different. Most monasteries are now a pile of rubble or a series of broken arches, covered in ivy, which have been exposed to the elements for over 400 years. The huge cathedrals and abbeys whose building took generations of dedication intended for Catholic worship have become Church of England establishments or parish churches. Like the monasteries, their artefacts and treasures were plundered.

This massive change of use and dedication was brought about by Henry VIII. After his final break with Rome, the passing of the Oath of Allegiance, the Act of Supremacy, the ending of his marriage to Catherine of Aragon and remarriage to Anne Boleyn, Henry embarked on a reign of terror to purge England of any association with Rome. In 1536 he started a series of investigations into how the monasteries were run. His surveyors were sent to value monasteries and enquire about the behaviour of the monks. Varying reports filtered back; some monks were having homosexual relationships, others had mistresses and had fathered children. This was enough to give Henry the power to close a monastery and either pay off or execute the monks. Some of the younger monks were allowed to go free but often they stood against Henry's men and bloody battles ensued.

Previous page:
The modern shrine at Walsingham continues to draw contemporary pilgrims to the small Norfolk town, just as that desecrated by Henry's followers drew the faithful in the years before the Reformation.
AA Photo Library

Right:
The modern shrine that commemorates the murder of Thomas à Becket at Canterbury Cathedral.
Ben May

Opposite:
An historically accurate reconstruction of the shrine of Thomas à Becket may be seen within 'The Canterbury Tales', along with a reproduction of the tomb of the Black Prince at Canterbury.
Heritage Projects (Canterbury) Ltd

The monasteries were plundered of all the goods, treasure and artefacts which, with the site, were passed to Henry, increasing his land ownership considerably. However, there were difficulties. In September 1536, Henry's men found the monks at Hexham Abbey were armed. At the same time there was revolt, in Louth, against the dissolution of the monasteries and the new religious laws being imposed. The Pilgrimage of Grace, as it became known, quickly spread through Lincolnshire, Yorkshire, Lancashire and northwards. Walsingham was the only town in the south to support the rebellion; London and the rest of the south remained loyal to the King. Eventually Henry was forced to pardon any rebel north of Doncaster.

In 1537, as part of the changes, Henry allowed the Bible to be printed in English and distributed for the first time. In 1526 William Tyndale translated the new Testament into English, but he himself was executed for heresy in 1536. Earlier, Henry had been unhappy about making the Bible available in English but eventually agreed to it as apart of the reforms, along with the enforcement of the Ten Articles. Keeping the Bible in Latin had made its reading accessible only to a small, educated elite. Making it more widely understood meant that people would be free to interpret it as they wished, not as someone else wanted them to. Like many politicians since, Henry was concerned about encouraging thought amongst the masses.

By 1538 Henry allowed the desecration of major Catholic shrines. The Walsingham shrines were moved to London; Richard of Chichester's bones were removed from Chichester cathedral and burnt; and Thomas à Becket's shrine at Canterbury (which had long been a place of pilgrimage for Henry) was desecrated, the bones removed and the jewels and pilgrims' gifts given to Henry.

By 1540 the dissolution of the monasteries was complete. Cromwell was replaced by Gardiner and Henry had met Katherine Howard. The country had seen their king behave in a deplorable way as he rooted out traitors, heretics and anyone who spoke against him or his decrees. Neighbours were asked to inform on each other, sometimes only doing so to save their own skin. Executions and burnings were commonplace in towns and villages throughout England. The Machiavellian Henry had all the characteristics of dictators before and since: determined to get his way no matter what the suffering. No deed was too terrible to commit if it brought about the result he wanted. England was, in 1540, a very different country from the one he had inherited in 1509.

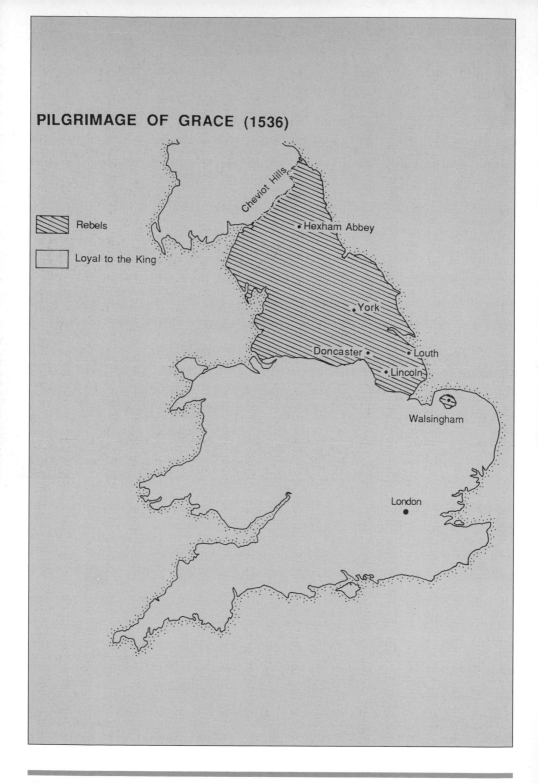

PILGRIMAGE OF GRACE (1536)

Rebels

Loyal to the King

Cheviot Hills

Hexham Abbey

York

Doncaster

Louth

Lincoln

Walsingham

London

Above:
The Pilgrimage of Grace, 1536.

Shrines

Walsingham

Shirehall Museum
Common Place
Little Walsingham
Norfolk NR22 6BP
1 Open from Maundy Thu–end of Sep, weekends in Oct
2 Yes
3 Yes

The shrine at Walsingham was one of three desecrated by Henry. The museum, in the heart of the town, has a gallery devoted to the shrine's history and the appalling suffering of the people during the Catholic purges.

Canterbury

Thomas à Becket's shrine in Canterbury Cathedral had long been a place of pilgrimage and consequently was very well endowed. Henry himself had visited it and prayed there on numerous occasions. However, in one of his most calculated attacks on Papal authority, he ordered its sacking and the removal of Becket's name from liturgical books.

Above:
Canterbury Cathedral was the location of the shrine to Thomas à Becket and the destination of many pilgrims. Henry's desire to expunge Catholicism from the country led to the desecration of the shrine.
Ben May

Above:
The cathedral at Chichester was another site where a medieval shrine was destroyed. This time Henry's followers reburied the body in a secret location.
AA Photo Library

Opposite:
The ruins of the 13th century Beaulieu Abbey in Hampshire looking across the cloisters to the Domus building. This was once the Lay Brothers' Apartments and is now used for events. An exhibition on monastic life at Beaulieu is contained on the ground floor of the building.
Beaulieu Abbey

Chichester

Richard of Chichester (1197–1253) was canonised in 1262 and his body enshrined in 1276 behind the high altar in Chichester Cathedral. The shrine was raided and the body reburied at a secret location, by Henry's men, in 1538.

Dales Countryside Museum
Station Yard
Hawes
North Yorkshire DL8 3NT
01969 667494
1 Apr–Oct
2 Yes
3 Yes
Exhibits at the museum document the enormous impact of the dissolution and other Tudor policies on the Dales and surrounding areas.

Commisioners

Between 1536 and 1540 Henry appointed Commissioners and Surveyors to oversee the suppression of the monasteries. They managed to close, demolish and plunder hundreds of monasteries, priories and abbeys. Most had stood for hundreds of years but met their end with Henry's single-minded and dictatorial campaign of destruction. Henry, as well as many commissioners, became immensely wealthy. Sir William Cavendish was a Commissioner for the dissolution, his fortune became the basis on which the Cavendish family eventually built Chatsworth in Derbyshire, themselves becoming the Dukes of Devonshire.

Remains

Whilst the remains of many monasteries disappeared long ago, others stand as mighty ruins of devotion and loyalty to God.

Beaulieu Abbey
The John Montagu Building
Beaulieu
Hampshire SO42 7ZN
01590 612345
1 All year
2 Yes
3 Yes
The Cistercian abbey was founded by King John in 1204. Henry stayed here in August 1510 on a journey to the south-west. However, the abbey was dissolved in 1538. The first Earl of Southampton, Thomas Wriothesley, bought it from Henry and turned the great gate house into a hunting lodge called Palace House. The estate and abbey ruins have passed, by direct descent, to the present owner, the third Lord Montagu of Beaulieu. There is an exhibition about monastic life at the abbey.

The Oxford Story
6 Broad Street
Oxford OX1 3AJ,
Oxon
01865 790055
1 All year
2 Yes
3 Nearby
Part of the Oxford Story shows Henry's desecration of many of the colleges which had been run by monastic orders. Towards the end of his life he founded five new professorships as well as making Cardinal's College King Henry VIII's College, now Christ Church.

The great Cistercian abbeys of Rievaulx, Byland and Fountains in North Yorkshire.
Rievaulx Abbey EH
Helmsley
North Yorkshire YO6 5LB
014396 228
1 All year
2 Yes. EH members free
3 Yes
The ruins of Rievaulx rise majestically in the wooded Rye Valley and are some of the finest examples of Early English architecture. The walls of the abbey church, covered with rows of pointed arches, still stand; the roof and windows are long gone. The extensive ruins point to the energy and wealth of this community of Cistercian monks, who made it one of the most influential abbeys in the north, and to Henry's act of vandalism. There is an exhibition about monastic life and the businesses run by the monks who lived here.

Opposite above:
The abbey gateway at Beaulieu with the famous stately home beyond.
AA Photo Library

Opposite below:
A diorama portraying a scene from the Oxford Story: on Henry's orders the contents of a monastic college are taken and catalogued.
The Oxford Story

Left:
The dramatic ruins of Rievaulx Abbey in North Yorkshire are amongst the most spectacular to be found in England.
English Heritage Photographic Library

Byland Abbey EH

Coxwold
near Thirsk
North Yorkshire YO6 4BD
013476 614
1 All year, closed Mon Oct–Mar
2 Yes. EH members free
3 Parking

The Byland monks moved to various sites before making this their permanent home. It became a large community, as the scale of the cloister and church reveal. The west front reveals good examples of early Gothic architecture with its huge, broken rose window. Much has been preserved, including tiled floors and seats for the lay brothers.

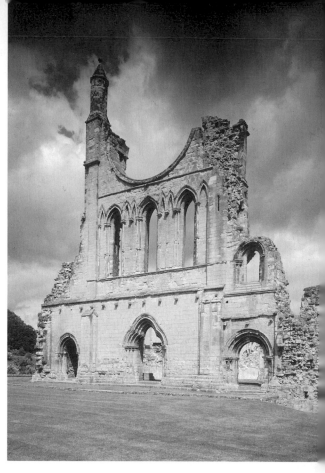

Fountains Abbey NT

Ripon
North Yorkshire HG3 4DY
01765 608888
1 All year
2 Yes. NT members free
3 Yes

Fountains Abbey was the wealthiest of the Yorkshire orders, owning wool-producing estates throughout the county. In the 16th century the tallest tower ever built by the Cistercians was erected at the end of the north transept. The vast remains of the community buildings stretch over a wide area, making it the largest monastic ruin in Britain. They include: the 300ft-long 'cellarium', the Chapter House, Warming House, many graves of the monks and a model in the visitor centre shows how the abbey would have looked prior to its dissolution in 1539.

Cleeve Abbey EH
Abbey Road
Washford
Somerset TA23 OPS
01984 40377
1 All year, closed Mon Oct–Mar
2 Yes. EH members free
3 Yes
The well-preserved ruins of the cloister buildings at Cleeve Abbey owe much to them being put to domestic use immediately after the dissolution. The great dining hall has floor tiles, carved wooden angels and wall paintings. A special exhibition recreates the lives of the 28 Cistercian monks and other lay brethren who lived here. At the time of dissolution it was valued at under £200.00.

St John's Gate
Museum of the Order of St John
St John's Gate
St John's Lane
Clerkenwell
London EC1M 4DA
0171 253 6644
1 Mon-Sat
2 Donation
3 No
The gatehouse to the Priory of the Knights of St John was built in 1504 and dissolved by Henry in 1540. It was the last monastic building to be dissolved by him and was given to Mary Tudor. The Priors of St John were temporal barons who sat on the Privy Council and acted as ambassadors to Henry. There is some Tudor architecture here as well as manuscripts and portraits of Henry in the museum.

Previous pages:
The well-preserved monastic buildings of Cleeve Abbey.
English Heritage Photographic Library

Right:
A warrant for the destruction of the priory church, Clerkenwell, from the Museum of the Order of St John.
Museum of the Order of St John

Above opposite:
Amongst the best-preserved of abbeys is that at Kirkstall near Leeds, in the Aire Valley.
The Ruined Abbeys of Britain

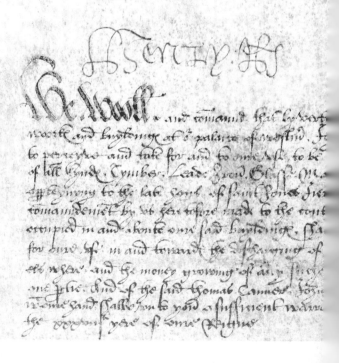

FROM THE NORTH-EAST,

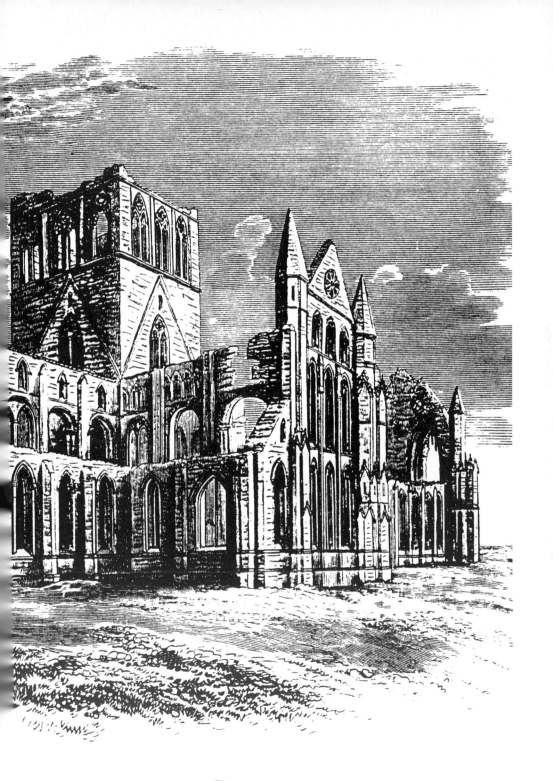

PPEARED BEFORE THE TOWER FELL.

Previous pages:
The ruined abbey at Whitby, situated on the cliffs above the town, is one of the most dramatic of all Britain's ruined abbeys. Whitby was one of the most important religious centres in British history; it was here in the mid-7th century that representatives of the Roman Catholic church and those of the Celtic Christian church (who represented the survival of Christianity in the British Isles after the Anglo-Saxon invaders had driven the native population to Ireland and Scotland following the withdrawal of the Romans in the 5th century) met in Synod to determine how the date of Easter should be calculated. The victory of the Catholic church led to a domination in England that was only to end with Henry VIII's break with Rome. The ruins at Whitby are significantly reduced from those illustrated. The central tower collapsed in the 19th century and further damage occurred during the past 100 years.
The Ruined Abbeys of Britain

Above:
Glastonbury today is perhaps best-known as the home of an annual music festival, but the ruined abbey acted as a focus for pilgrims of an earlier faith. By tradition St Joseph of Arimathea, in whose tomb the body of Jesus Christ was buried after the crucifixion, was exiled and found his way to Glastonbury with the Holy Grail. Amongst the most significant ruins at Glastonbury are the abbey kitchens and St Joseph's Chapel.
The Ruined Abbeys of Britain

Other Sites

Devon
Torre Abbey in Torquay was founded in 1196 as a monastery for the Premonstratersian Order of Canons. It was suppressed in 1539 and the church demolished. Simon Rede, the last abbot, became Vicar of Townstall near Dartmouth; the other canons were pensioned off. Rede received a pension of £64.00 per annum and the others between £3.00 and £8.00. The remains comprise the most complete surviving monastic buildings in Devon.

Dorset
Jason Tregonwell, Henry's lawyer in the divorce proceedings, was also a Commissioner for the dissolution of the monasteries. He oversaw the surrender of Milton Abbey in Blandford Forum in 1539 and bought the entire estate for £1,000.00. He and his family lived in the monastic buildings and church for 200 years; the abbot's hall and abbey church, built in 1498, still remain.

Hereford and Worcester
In 1085 Benedictine monks from Worcester Priory founded Great Malvern Priory on land belonging to Westminster Abbey. Henry, who visited the priory with his parents and Prince Arthur in 1501, gave the window in the north transept. He would have entered through the still-standing church and gatehouse. The church was saved from destruction by the local people when the priory was dissolved in 1539; it is now the parish church.

The first monastery at Leominster was founded in AD660 and later became an abbey of nuns which was dissolved in 1046. In 1123 a Cluniac priory was founded as a cell of Reading; this was dissolved in 1539. Two naves were used by the secular clergy to form the parish church.

The stone from the demolished parts of the priory were used for secular buildings like the mansion house and hospital. The abbot of the mother house at Reading, Hugh Farrington, resisted the dissolution and was executed. The last prior was replaced by a lay official who handed the monastery over to the Crown.

Although little remains of Bordesley Abbey in Redditch, excavations have revealed how it was dismantled. Tiles removed from the floor have left their impressions, the north wall was demolished to allow carts in to remove the tiles, lead and glass and piles of rubble were left until excavations began in 1969.

Middlesex
The estate at Headstone Manor in Harrow was owned by the Archbishops of Canterbury but was passed to Henry at the dissolution. He owned it for one week before selling it to Lord North.

Norfolk
St Andrews and Blackfriars Halls in Norwich are unique in that they form the most complete surviving friary complex in England. By selling all the friary buildings to the city for £81.00 Henry ensured their survival. The deed of sale is in the Norfolk County Records Office.

The ruins of Castle Acre Priory represent the best surviving remnants of a Cluniac house in England. At the time of its dissolution, there were only 11 monks in residence.

Oxfordshire

Sulgrave Manor
Manor Road
Sulgrave
Banbury
Oxon OX17 2SD
01295 760205
1 Mar, Nov, Dec,
weekends only; Apr-Oct
Thu-Tue.
2 Yes
3 Yes
In 1538 Henry acquired
the Manor of Sulgrave
with the dissolution of
the Priory of St Andrews
in Northampton. The
following year he sold it
to Lawrence Washington for £324.14s.10d. Washington was Mayor of Northampton and
a leading member of the Wool Guilds in London and Northampton. His uncle was Lord
John Spencer of Althorpe. The house was built in 1539 and its rooms are furnished with
pieces from the Tudor period.

Shropshire

There is still much evidence of Tudor architecture in Shrewsbury, its position near the
Welsh border making it important in national affairs. The abbey was founded in 1083 by
Benedictine monks. On 24 January 1540 14 monks, three novices and the abbot were
pensioned off. The abbot received a pension of £80.00 per annum. The monastery had
enjoyed a reputation of good behaviour, observance and scholarship having provided
two chancellors of Oxford University and a school in Shrewsbury. The citizens prayed,
unsuccessfully, that Henry would restore the school. The abbey and the land passed
through various owners and much of the fabric was used in buildings elsewhere.
However, the church became the church for the parish of the Holy Cross.
Also in Shropshire are the ruined abbeys at Much Wenlock and Buildwas.

Suffolk

Bury St Edmunds possessed until the dissolution one of the most important Benedictine
monasteries in England and the ruins are impressive. Amongst these are the two
gateways which controlled access to the monastery precincts. Although much of the
abbey church was demolished the west front survives in part with, curiously, a number
of houses built into it. The present cathedral, originally the church of St James, was
largely built during the reign of Henry VIII , although Edward VI contributed funds
towards its construction, and is a fine example of Perpendicular architecture.

West Sussex

The Priest House at West Hoathly was built in the early 15th century by the Cluniac
Priory of Lewes. In 1538 the land belonging to the priory was taken by Henry and given
to Thomas Cromwell until his death, when it was used as part of Anne of Cleves' divorce
settlement. The house still stands and is a good example of a timber-framed construction
of the period.

West Yorkshire

In 1537 Temple Newsam House, Leeds, was confiscated by Henry from Thomas Lord Darcy for his part in the Pilgrimage of Grace. In 1544 Henry granted it to his niece Margaret, Countess of Lennox.

Wiltshire

After the dissolution, Henry sold Lacock Abbey (NT) to Sir William Sharington who made it his home, much of which still exists.

Wales

Tintern Abbey, Chepstow, Gwent — a Cistercian abbey founded in 1131, closed and stripped of valuables in 1536.

Westminster Abbey

The Benedictine abbey, where Henry's parents are buried, was dissolved and the abbey became a cathedral church. Later, Henry's children, Edward, Mary and Elizabeth were to be buried here.

York

The York Story

St Mary's Church
Coppergate Centre
York YO1 1RN
North Yorkshire
01904 628632
1 All year
2 Yes
3 No

The York Story explains the long history of this fascinating city which had been a centre of government for the north. However, Henry thoroughly pursued his cause in the city. In 1535 he pillaged the church of St Mary Castlegate and closed the monastic houses at Holy Trinity Priory and Clementhorpe Nunnery. This left him weak and open to the dissent of the Pilgrimage of Grace, which the citizens of York keenly joined.

York Minster

Dean's Park
York YO1 2JD
North Yorkshire
01904 625308
1 All year
2 Donation
3 No

In 1514 Henry appointed Thomas Wolsey as Archbishop of York and, at that time, any possibility of change seemed remote. Wolsey never lived in York but ran the post through a number of resident deputies so the Minster remained fairly independent. However, Archbishop Lee visited in 1534 to discover more of the management of its affairs. Apart from a few minor anomalies he could find little that required change. By 1539 Thomas Cranmer was setting up new cathedral foundations without prebendaries, who were plentiful at York, and whom he regarded as unnecessary, expensive and idle.

Opposite above:
Sulgrave manor house.
Blinkhorn-Haynes Photography

Following pages:
A detail of the ruined west front at Tintern Abbey.
Peter Waller

But York did manage to survive with little change although it did lose much of its treasure to the Crown. The Minster Library's History of Binding Collection holds a copy of *Svmmaria in Evangelia et Epistolas,* printed in 1536 and inscribed 'from the library of Henry VIII'.

Lincoln
Lincoln Cathedral
Lincoln LN2 1PZ
Lincolnshire
01522 544544
1 All year
2 Donation
3 Nearby
The diocese of Lincoln was the largest in medieval England, stretching from the Humber to the Thames, and this great cathedral stood resplendent at its helm. In 1536 the people of Lincoln were outraged by Henry's acts and the subsequent Lincolnshire Risings resulted in many deaths, hangings and imprisonments. Twenty-one ringleaders were executed. Henry regarded the county as unruly and when he visited in 1541, on his way to Grimsthorpe (see page 153), he was very vocal about his feelings. In 1542 the rich shrines and chantries were stripped of their gold and assets. When Henry visited, the cathedral and minster yard would have been much as they are today, dominated by the enormous cathedral spire. Inside is the chantry chapel of Henry's confessor, Bishop Longland.

William Tyndale's 1526 Translation of the New Testament
Three thousand copies of Tyndale's translation of the New Testament were originally printed at Worms in 1526. Two remain, one at St Paul's Cathedral with 71 missing pages and a complete one at The British Museum. Tyndale was burnt as a heretic in 1536.

Canterbury Cathedral
Canterbury
Kent CT1 2EH
01227 762864
1 All year
2 No
3 No
Canterbury Cathedral was often visited by Henry whilst in Kent and *en route* to Dover. He prayed at Thomas à Becket's shrine until he ordered its desecration in what was regarded, by the Pope, as a most despicable act against Christendom. The Archbishops of Canterbury had been important members of his court and were often placed in difficult positions of loyalty to Henry and the Pope.

The Canterbury Tales
23 Hawks Lane
Canterbury
Kent CT1 2NU
01227 454888
1 All year
2 Yes
3 No
This walk-through exhibition describes Canterbury at the time of Chaucer and the journeys of pilgrims to the shrine of Thomas à Becket in the cathedral. The shrine has been carefully reconstructed to show it as it would have been before its destruction.

CHAPTER 11:
THE LANDOWNER

At the end of his life Henry was a wealthy landowner and many of his estates still belong to the Crown. He spent his early years in palaces at Eltham, Greenwich and Richmond and had no qualms, on his accession, about acquiring more properties or building new ones. On his death he owned 67 houses, a vast increase on the 23 he had inherited. However, Henry's children, after his death, were eager to dispose of much of the property and by 1649 only 23 (by co-incidence) houses remained.

Like his father, Henry VIII needed the revenue from the properties but the various wars and skirmishes in Europe quickly used up much of it. In 1511 he appointed a small court of General Surveyors of Crown Lands, accountable to the Exchequer. This body was the first Government body concerned with income from Crown lands and was the basis of the Crown Estate.

Like many of his European counterparts he embarked on numerous building projects, making him the greatest builder-king England has ever known. Palaces like Nonsuch were based on François I's new palace at Fontainebleau which had been influenced by Florentine designs. Henry knew what was necessary to be a sophisticated, modern, European monarch.

On his accession he inherited a number of partially finished buildings from his father. With Wolsey's help he completed these, altered some and bought more. In 1520 a vast temporary palace was built at the Field of the Cloth of Gold. However, Henry was not really interested in building until 1529 when, due to Wolsey's demise, he was forced to become involved in the construction programme. With Wolsey's fall he acquired Hampton Court. The increasing fall of other courtiers made him the recipient of more buildings and estates.

After Wolsey's downfall, Henry embarked on his building projects with the same enthusiasm and thoroughness he used for purging Papists, Lutherans and heretics and suppressing the people. Maybe, through these building projects, he felt able to control his environment, creating just what he wanted. The dissolution of the Monasteries (1536–40) made him very wealthy. Their suppression and eviction of the monks meant that he acquired land, buildings,

Previous page:
The Great Hall at Hampton Court which was used by Henry VIII.
© *Historic Royal Palaces*

Below:
The west front of Hampton Court Palace.
© *Historic Royal Palaces*

Opposite:
The painted closet of Cardinal Wolsey at Hampton Court.
© *Historic Royal Palaces*

artefacts and building materials. Stone from a plundered building would be transported to Henry's latest site.

Henry was a multi-faceted man, designing palaces, houses, forts, armour and jewellery, as well as establishing educational foundations. He did not rely on designers, but did the work himself, drawing the plans and often managing the workforce. Simon Thurley[1] describes the determination with which he used builders, craftsmen and administrators. It was not unusual for him to alter plans at the last minute

and expect people to work long hours changing what they had done earlier. Like many wealthy clients, Henry wanted his buildings to impress.

Palaces and houses had, by necessity, to be large. Whenever the king or queen stayed anywhere they were accompanied by an entourage of hundreds of courtiers, advisers and servants. If a foreign dignitary accompanied them, that entourage too would require accommodation. Until 1530 the king and queen had separate apartments, one directly on the floor above the other. When Jane Seymour arrived the king and queen's apartments were on the same level.

In addition to buildings the Crown owned huge areas of open land like Richmond Park and Epping Forest. In his early years Henry was a keen hunter, spending most of the day time on a horse and leaving Wolsey to run the country.

Property is yet another example of Henry's impact on English history, whether it be the massive destruction of the monasteries or the huge construction projects of palaces, houses and defensive battlements. No monarch has changed the environment to such an extent as Henry VIII. Near most towns and villages in England there is some physical example of his property development — a ruin or a building.

Tudor architecture has, this century, been revived. Like all revivals this has meant taking certain elements from the original, distilling them and mixing them with modern requirements. In the 1930s estates of semi-detached houses were built in suburbs. In essence this meant white-fronted houses with dark beams across the gable ends, tall brick chimneys and leaded windows; inside three bedrooms, lounge and dining room replaced the endless chambers of a 16th-century palace. The 1990s equivalent is a house built of small bricks, with tall chimneys, an inglenook fireplace and central heating. Tudor Closes and Tudor Vales appear on suburban maps throughout England.

The Thames was an invaluable transport route for Henry from Greenwich via the City and Hampton Court to Windsor. In London Henry moved around between Bridewell, The Tower (then used as a royal residence as well as a prison), Whitehall, St James's Palace and Hampton Court. In the summer he would escape the heat and disease of London by going on a progress. These trips to places like Enfield and Woking would take weeks, the entourage maybe staying at six different locations.

ACQUIRED FROM:

Buckingham in 1521
Thornbury, Penshurst Place

Wolsey in 1529
Hampton Court, The Moor, York Place (Whitehall), Tyttenhanger, Esher

Cranmer in 1537
Charing, Otford, Knole

Marquess of Exeter in 1538
West Horsley

Sir Nicholas Carew in 1539
Beddington

Other houses were exchanged and between 1516 and 1536 he bought four. Henry also owned the homes of his children.

HE BUILT:

Nonsuch,

Bridewell,

St James' Palace

[1]The Royal Palaces of Tudor England, Simon Thurley, Yale 1993

Above opposite:
The Museum at Richmond-upon-Thames includes models of a number of buildings associated with Henry in the area which no longer survive. This is a model of the Palace built at Richmond, viewed from the river, side. Note the barge; river travel was by far the most comfortable and quickest form of getting from Richmond into London and, as shown in the film *A Man For All Seasons*, both the monarch and his subjects used the river frequently.
Museum of Richmond

Opposite:
The model of Shene Charterhouse, destroyed in the dissolution of the monasteries, as displayed in the Museum of Richmond.
Museum of Richmond

To Sr John Shaw Bart
Proprietor of this Palace
This Prospect is humbly Inscrib'd by
his most Obedient Servts
Sam.l & Nath.l Buck.

ACE, IN THE COUNTY OF KENT.

Anthony Beck Bishop of Durham having obtain'd the Manor & Capital Mansion of the Vesci's here, converted it into a Palace, which he gave to Eleanor Consort of K: Edw: I. Queen Isabel Consort of K: Edw: II was deliver'd of John surnam'd of Eltham at this Palace. K: Edw: III enter= tain'd the Kings of France, Scotland, & Armenia, at ye same time here; and this was K: Hen: VI usual place of Residence. K: Edw: IV who laid out large Sums in ye Repairs, entertain'd 2000 persons in ye great Hall. K: Hen: VIII built the fair Front towards ye Moat. His Successors as well as Predecessors spent most of their hours of pleasure here till Greenwich grew up when this was neglected. Part of ye Manor of Eltham was granted by K: Ch: II to Sr John Shaw Bart. for his firm Attachment to the Royal cause, who by purchase of the remainder from Col: Panton & Sr Nichs Crisp became sole Proprietor; as is at this time his Grandson the Worthy Sr John Shaw Bart.   S. & N. Buck. delin et Sculp.t 1735.

PROBABLE ORIGINAL APPEARANCE FROM THE SOUTH-EAST

Hampton Court Palace

East Molesey
Surrey KT8 9AU
0181 781 9500
1 All year
2 Yes
3 Yes

Hampton Court Palace is the home most associated with Henry and indeed there is a lot here relating to him. The site of the palace was leased to Thomas Wolsey in 1514 who undertook a massive building programme, making it one of his homes whilst Lord Chancellor. However, his demise in 1529 meant he had to forfeit it to Henry who immediately began further rebuilding and extension programmes. Situated on the banks of the Thames, it was easily accessible by boat from London and became Henry's main home, and the only one capable of housing the entire court. It was here that Jane Seymour gave birth to Edward and where she died. The scale of the palace necessitated the building of huge kitchens which are now open to the public. There are occasional demonstrations of the huge ovens roasting meat as well as cake decoration and other aspects of food preparation.

In Henry's Great Hall there may be Tudor dancing and entertainment by a lively court jester, whilst the chapel and Wolsey's Closet give an indication of the wealth of the Court.

Subsequent monarchs have lived at Hampton Court and the palace bears the marks of their building programmes and styles. When walking from the West Gate, one sees the low brick building designed by Wolsey, whilst on the eastern side there is a baroque façade built by Wren.

Museum of Richmond

Old Town Hall
Whittaker Avenue
Richmond
Surrey TW9 1TP
0181 332 1141
1 Nov-Apr Tue-Sat, May-Oct Tue-Sun.
2 Yes
3 Weekends only

Richmond Palace, situated on The Green where jousting took place, was often used by Henry in the early part of the reign. The remains of the palace are now in private ownership. However, the museum does have a very detailed model of it and Shene Charterhouse, which was destroyed during the dissolution. Part of Anne of Cleves' divorce settlement was Richmond Palace, where she lived with an annual income of £3,000.

Greenwich Borough Museum

232 Plumstead High Street
London SE18 1JT
0181 855 3240
1 All year; closed Mon morning, all day Wed and Sun.
2 No
3 No

Henry was born at Greenwich, but much of the Tudor evidence has been supplanted by later developments. The museum charts the borough's history with emphasis on the palace and dockyard.

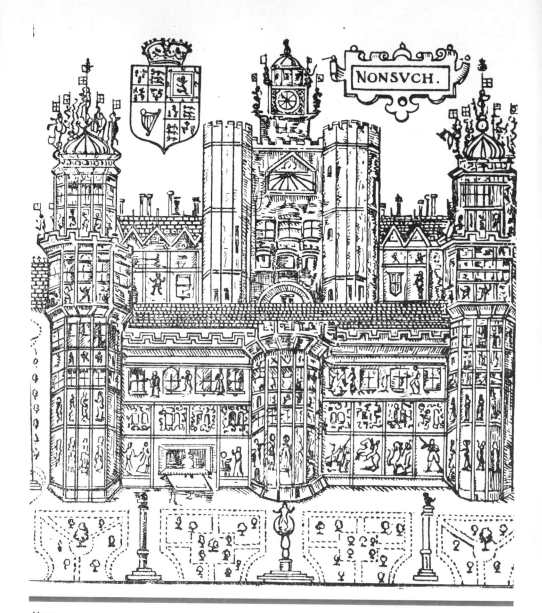

Above:
The Palace of Nonsuch was built by Henry in imitation of the French palace at Fontainebleau. The palace has been destroyed, although fragments can be seen in various locations. This engraving of the palace is part of the collection of the Museum of London.
© *Museum of London*

Opposite above:
A gargoyle lion's head, looted from Merton Abbey and found in the rubble of the palace's foundations, is also on display at Bourne Hall Museum.
© *Bourne Hall Museum*

Opposite:
The Nonsuch chest is one of many items on display at Bourne Hall Museum about Henry's destroyed palace. The inlaid woodwork is supposed to reflect the architecture of the palace.
© *Bourne Hall Museum*

Eltham Palace EH
Court Yard
Eltham
London SE9
0181 854 2242
1 Thu and Sun only — 10am-6pm summer months;
10am-4pm winter
2 Yes. EH members free
3 Contact in advance
Henry VIII rebuilt the Chancellor's Lodgings, which, unfortunately is not open to the public. In 1527 he spent Christmas at Eltham instead of at Greenwich.

Queen Elizabeth's Hunting Lodge
Rangers Road
Chingford
London E4 7QH
0181 529 6681
1 All year Wed-Sun
2 Yes
3 Yes
Epping Forest is now all that remains of the once huge Royal Forest of Waltham which stretched from Epping to Colchester and down to the Thames. Deer were protected for hunting and clearings made for them to give birth and feed. Even if someone owned land within a Royal Forest he could not kill deer or fell trees without Royal consent.

Queen Elizabeth's Hunting Lodge was built in 1543 to a very high standard for Henry who had, by then, become ill and too fat to ride. From the top floor or 'Great Standing' of the lodge he could watch the hunt across Chingford Plain and shoot the occasional deer himself.

Nonsuch Palace
Henry based the building of Nonsuch Palace on Fontainebleau which had recently been built by François in France. He wanted to demonstrate that he was a European monarch by using, like François, guilders and craftsmen from Italy. Although the palace disappeared long ago, remnants of it can be found in various locations:

Bourne Hall Museum
Spring Street
Ewell
Surrey KT17 1UF
0181 394 1734
1 All year, closed Sun
2 No
3 Yes
The museum houses an exhibition about Nonsuch which includes photographs, documents, stonework and pottery from excavations completed in 1959.

Loseley House
Loseley Park
Guildford
Surrey GU3 1HS
011483 304440
1 May-Oct, Wed-Sat
2 Yes
3 Yes
Loseley Manor was bought by Sir Christopher More in 1508 when he was an Exchequer Official to Henry VII. He lived in a house in the grounds and it was his son Sir William More, a relation by marriage of Sir Thomas More, who built the present house in 1562. Sir William was a close associate of Elizabeth I who stayed here on many occasions.

Inside the house there are portraits of Anne Boleyn and Sir Thomas More as well as pictures from Henry VIII's banqueting tents. Nonsuch is well represented by panelling and furniture. Some panelling bears Catherine Parr's initials (Nonsuch was built for her), another piece bears Henry's portcullis motif and there are some beautifully carved *trompe l'oeil* panels. Sir Thomas More's bedroom contains furniture of later periods.

St James's Palace

Although not open to the public as it is still much used as a Royal residence, the palace is clearly visible at the end of St James's Street in central London. It was built by Henry around 1533, whilst married to Anne Boleyn. Their initials, entwined in a love knot, are carved in the stonework. The palace was built in a park of 160 acres which Henry acquired from the demoted Wolsey, and was to form part of the Palace of Whitehall complex.

HM Tower of London

London EC3N 4AB
0171 709 0765
1 All year
2 Yes
3 No

Traditionally the Tower had been both a royal residence and prison. The Medieval Palace has been restored to give an indication of life at the Tower in Henry's time. Anne Boleyn and Katherine Howard were executed on Tower Green and Thomas More, Fisher and many others were imprisoned here before execution on Tower Hill, now Trinity Green. The Royal Armouries, within the Tower precinct, contain a vast array of Henry's armour and weapons.

Opposite:
The north front of Loseley Park in Surrey.
English Life Publications Ltd

Above:
St James' Palace.
AA Photo Library

Left:
The great hall at Loseley Park.
English Life Publications Ltd

Kent

Henry often passed through Kent on his way to Dover and then France. He made numerous visits to Canterbury Cathedral to pray at Thomas à Becket's shrine before ordering its desecration; he acquired many homes in the county and built defences along its coast to defend it from invasion.

Knole NT
Knole
Sevenoaks
Kent
01732 450608
1 Apr-Oct, Wed-Sun
2 Yes. NT members free
3 Yes
Knole is now the largest private house in England, having its beginnings in 1456 and being extended, in 1603, by Thomas Sackville to whose descendents it still belongs.

Knole did not escape Henry's attentions. Thomas Bourchier, Archbishop of Canterbury, bought the estate in 1456 and built the house. On his death in 1486 it passed to the See of Canterbury. Henry VIII appropriated it in Cranmer's period as Archbishop, and greatly enlarged it. Plasterwork ceilings, marble chimney pieces and carved wooden panelling all survive. The gatehouse on the West Front and some of the buildings in the Green Court were built to house Henry's enormous court. He stayed at Knole in 1541 whilst on his way from Eltham to Penshurst via Otford and Knole. Inside there are many rooms of the period but, like many places with numerous associations over the years, the furniture and artefacts are from various times and origins. There are, however, portraits, after Holbein, of Henry and his family.

Penshurst Place
Penshurst
Tonbridge
Kent TN11 8DG
01892 870307

1 End Mar - beginning Oct everyday. Weekends only in Mar and Oct

2 Yes

3 Yes

In 1519 Henry visited Penshurst Place which was then owned by Edward Stafford, the third Duke of Buckingham. Stafford went to a lot of expense to entertain and feed Henry, spending £2,800 (the equivalent of £870,000 today). By 1521 Buckingham had fallen out of favour and was executed for treason on Tower Hill. The house then passed to the Crown and Henry owned it until his death in 1547. He appointed Thomas Boleyn to manage it and used it frequently whilst courting Boleyn's sisters, Mary and Anne, who lived nearby at Hever Castle.

On Henry's death the house passed to his son, Edward VI, who gave it to Sir William Sidney in 1552. Sidney had been a loyal servant to Henry having fought at the Battle of Flodden after which he was knighted. In 1520 he accompanied Henry to the Field of the Cloth of Gold. By 1538 he was Chamberlain to the Prince of Wales but Penshurst was his most important grant. The house and family had close connections with all Henry's children.

The north wing of the house was built by Sir Henry Sidney and finished in 1585 and provides a good example of a building of the period. In the crypt an exhibition about the Sydney family documents their history through the Tudor period to the present. Elsewhere there are arms and armour, furniture and paintings from the period. There are portraits of Henry and his family as well as numerous ones of the Sidney family and associates.

Nearby Penshurst church contains a small brass dedicated to Thomas Boleyn.

Opposite:
The front at Knole.
The National Trust

Top:
The painted staircase at Knole.
The National Trust

Above:
The Baron's Hall at Penshurst Place.
Penshurst Place

Leeds Castle
Maidstone
Kent ME17 1PL
01622 765400
1 All year
2 Yes
2 Yes
Leeds Castle stands dramatically surrounded by a wide moat full of water. Henry VIII was its most famous landowner and spent huge amounts of money on it; he retained its defences for, even so far inland, he feared a French invasion and visited often. In 1512 he appointed Sir Henry Guildford as Constable and Parker of Leeds. Guildford was also a Member of Parliament, Comptroller of the Royal Household and, in 1520, organiser of the English party at the Field of the Cloth of Gold.

Henry undertook the most major of all improvements at the castle. He put bay windows into the Royal apartments and repaired all the rooms. The Royal maids-of-honour, including Anne Boleyn, were housed in the newly renovated Maiden's Tower. After the failed invasion of France in 1544 Henry returned to Leeds with the Privy Council where the Imperial Ambassadors left and were not replaced. The castle is full of associations with Henry, including portraits, busts and his banqueting hall.

See also Hever Castle, page 43, and Sudeley Castle, page 50.

Opposite:
An aerial view of
Leeds Castle in Kent.
*Leeds Castle
Foundation*

Above left:
Catherine of Aragon's
Missal is one of many
items relating to the
reign of Henry VIII on
display at Leeds
Castle. A Missal
contains all the
Catholic prayers and
rites for Masses
throughout the year.
*Leeds Castle
Foundation*

Above right:
Anne Boleyn's jewel
box is also on display
at Leeds Castle.
*Leeds Castle
Foundation*

Left:
A portrait of Henry
VIII painted on wood
by an unknown artist
from the collection at
Leeds Castle.
*Leeds Castle
Foundation*

Following page:
Henry VIII's
Banqueting Hall at
Leeds Castle.
*Leeds Castle
Foundation*

Grimsthorpe and Drummond Castle Trust Ltd
Grimsthorpe
Bourne
Lincolnshire PE10 0NB
01778 32205
1 Easter Sun and Mon, Bank Holidays and Sun from 30 May-11 Sep
2 Yes
3 Yes
Henry VIII granted the house to William, 10th Baron Willoughby de Eresby on his
marriage to Maria de Salinas, a Lady in Waiting and cousin of Catherine of Aragon. In
1537 he granted it again to the Duke of Suffolk, Charles Brandon, who had earlier
married his sister Mary, the French Queen. After Mary's death, Suffolk married
Katherine Willoughby de Eresby, daughter of William and Maria. During the
Lincolnshire Uprising which started the Pilgrimage of Grace, Suffolk commanded the
King's army against the rebels. Henry and his court stayed at Grimsthorpe in 1541 on
the way to York to meets James V. It was here that Katherine Howard's adultery became
apparent. Alterations, using stone from Vaudey Abbey, were made to the house to
accommodate Henry's court. The de Eresby family still live at Grimsthorpe and inside
there are paintings of Henry as well as furniture of the period.

Rockingham Castle
Market Harborough
Leicestershire LE16 8TH
01536 770240
1 Easter-Sep Sun and Thu Bank Holiday Mon and Tue in Aug.
2 Yes
3 Yes
This Norman castle is situated on a hilltop giving it good surveillance of the surrounding
five counties. In 1544 Henry granted it to Edward Watson who converted it from a
defensive castle into a home. The fine Tudor hall has furniture and a huge fireplace from
the period as well as a portrait of François from the Field of the Cloth of Gold, a signed
letter from Henry to the Abbot of Peterborough and a portrait of Jane Seymour.

Previous page:
The exterior of Rockingham Castle.
Rockingham Castle

Above:
The great hall at Rockingham Castle showing the fine Tudor fireplace.
Rockingham Castle

CHAPTER 12:
DEATH

The last 11 years of Henry's life were fraught with ill health. A serious fall from his horse in 1536 left a bad sore on one leg which never properly healed and he had to abandon his great love, hunting. His increasingly enormous appetite and lack of exercise resulted in a waist measurement of 56in (1.4m) and made walking very difficult, latterly impossible. Popular culture likes to claim he had syphilis which was common, although in Henry's case never proven. Probably Anne Boleyn, and certainly Katherine Howard, hinted at his increasing lack of libido. His marriage to Catherine Parr was one of convenience and respect for her maternal and managerial skills rather than of great passion.

Despite his ill health and obesity he was determined to go to France in 1544 to lead the army and tried to negotiate peace with François. His advisers did not want him there; he was a great responsibility and had to be hauled onto a horse. However he did go, only to find Charles of Spain had negotiated a secret peace treaty leaving Henry at war with both of them. The armour belonging to him in the Royal Armouries gives an indication of his gigantic size, height and width; small wonder few dared to disagree with him.

By 1546 he was concerned by Catherine's Protestantism and nearly sent her to the Tower. He did, however, send the Protestant reformer Anne Askew, Norfolk and his son, Surrey. Surrey was beheaded in early January 1547 and Norfolk was to be executed but in fact was reprieved after Henry's death.

On 27 January Henry became very ill at Whitehall. Cranmer visited him as his last confessor and he died in the early hours of the next morning. Although his court had been expecting his death they were stunned, keeping it secret for a few days.

Henry was buried alongside his most loved wife, Jane Seymour, at St George's Chapel, Windsor. His son, Edward VI succeeded him, followed by his daughters Mary Tudor and Elizabeth I through whom the Tudor dynasty lasted until 1603.

Previous page:
A bust of Henry VIII as displayed at Leeds Castle.
Leeds Castle Foundation

Right:
St Georges Chapel at Windsor Castle where King Henry VIII lies buried alongside his favourite wife Jane Seymour.
AA Picture Library

Opposite:
Henry VIII's gateway at Windsor Castle.
AA Picture Library

St George's Chapel
Windsor Castle
Windsor
Berkshire SL4 1NJ
01753 831118
1 All year
2 Yes
3 Nearby
Edward IV began to build St George's Chapel in 1475, Henry VII added the nave and stone-vaulted ceiling and Henry VIII completed the building in 1528. The result is one of the best examples of late medieval gothic architecture. Generations of monarchs are buried here including Henry, alongside Jane Seymour.

Plays and Films

The life of Henry VIII has provided material for numerous plays and films:

Henry VIII by William Shakespeare
On the first performance of *Henry VIII*, by Fletcher and Shakespeare, at the Globe
Theatre, a prop cannon ignited and burnt the thatched roof of the theatre. The play is
now rarely performed. In the Prologue, Shakespeare describes, succinctly, its basis:

> I come no more to make you laugh. Things now
> That bear a weighty and a serious brow,
> Sad, high, and working, full of state and woe,
> Such noble scenes as draw the eye to flow,
> We now present. Those that can pity here
> May, if they think it well, let fall a tear;
> The subject will deserve it. Such as give
> Their money out of hope they may believe
> May here find truth too....
> ....Only they
> That come to hear a merry, bawdy play,
> A noise of targets, or to see a fellow
> In a long motley coat guarded with yellow,
> Will be deceived; ....
> ....Think ye see
> The very persons of our noble story
> As they were living; think you see them great,
> And followed with the general throng and sweat
> Of thousand friends: then, in a moment, see
> How soon this mightiness meets misery.
> And if you can be merry then, I'll say
> A man may weep upon his wedding day.

The Private Life of Henry VIII
Alexander Korda directed this film in 1933; it is regarded by many as the classic film
about Henry and starred Charles Laughton, Robert Donat and Merle Oberon.

Henry VIII and his Six Wives
Made in 1972, this film is based on one of the same name made in 1932. This later
edition was directed by Waris Hussein and starred Keith Michell, Jane Asher, Charlotte
Rampling and Lynne Frederick.

Anne of the Thousand Days
This film is based on the divorce of Catherine of Aragon and Anne Boleyn's short time as
queen. Directed by Charles Jarrott and starring Richard Burton, it was produced in 1969.

A Man for All Seasons
This was written as a play by Robert Bolt, who dealt with the life of and moral crises
faced by Sir Thomas More. The equally successful film was directed by Fred Zinnemann
in 1966 starring Paul Scofield, Wendy Hiller, Susannah York and Orson Welles.

Music
Henry VIII was a talented and skilled musician both as a composer and instrumentalist.
Although the writing of 'Greensleeves' has been attributed to him, there is no evidence

for this. Henry's compositions are still played by ensembles specialising in Renaissance music.

Victorian music-halls throughout England rang out with the words of the song 'I'm 'enery the eighth I am'.

Poetry

Two poets, Sir Thomas Wyatt and Henry Howard, Earl of Surrey, worked closely as advisors to Henry. Wyatt was a diplomat who accompanied Henry on missions to France. He was imprisoned in the Tower on suspicion of having been one of Anne Boleyn's lovers but was later released. In 1541 he received a Royal Pardon after having been charged with treason. He died of natural causes in 1542.

Henry Howard was a close friend of Henry's illegitimate son, Henry Fitzroy. He was suspected of siding with the rebels in the Pilgrimage of Grace and was imprisoned as a result. He joined Charles V's army, fighting with Rome and as a result was charged with treason in England and executed in 1547.

Both men wrote beautiful poetry which is available in:
Silver Poets of the Sixteenth Century, edited by Douglas Brooks-Davies, Everyman.

Bibliography and Further Reading

Philippe Aries, *Centuries of Childhood,*
Penguin 1973

L. Black, *The Love Letters of Henry the Eighth,*
Blandford Press 1933

Robert Bolt, *A Man for All Seasons,*
1960

D. Brooks-Davies,Ed, *Silver Poets of the Sixteenth Century,*
Everyman 1992

David Hugh Farmer, *The Oxford Dictionary of Saints,*
Clarendon Press 1980

Valerie Fildes, *Breast Feeding in Tudor and Stuart England, Midwives Chronicle*
June 1987.

B. Fletcher, *A History of Architecture on the Comparative Method,*
Athlone Press 1967

Antonia Fraser, *The Six Wives of Henry VIII,*
Weidenfeld and Nicholson 1993

E. H. Gombrich, *The Story of Art,*
Phaidon 1972

John Hale, *Renaissance Europe 1480–1520,*
Fontana 1971

John Hale, *The Civilization of Europe in the Renaissance,*
Harper Collins 1993

Henry VIII, Letters and Papers, Foreign and Domestic of the Reign of Henry VIII,
Vols 1 –21, Public Record Office

Ralph Houlbrooke, *The English Family 1450–1700,* Longman 1984

Niccolo Machiavelli, *The Prince,*
Penguin Classic 1981

Thomas More, *Utopia,*
Penguin Classic 1979

Lewis Mumford, *The City in History,*
Pelican 1979

Nikolaus Pevsner, *The Buildings of England,*
series by county,
Penguin 1951 onwards

R. B. Pugh, *The Crown Estate, An Historical Essay,*
HMSO 1960

Jasper Ridley, *Henry VIII,*
Constable 1984

Jane Roberts, *Holbein and the Court of Henry VIII, Drawings and Miniatures from the Royal Library, Windsor Castle,*
National Galleries of Scotland 1993

W. Shakespeare, *Henry VIII,*
New Penguin Edition 1971

Sarah Snowdon, *Trends in Infant Feeding in Early Modern England, Midwives Chronicle*
December 1993

Byrne M. S. Clare, *The Letters of King Henry VIII,*
Cassell 1936

State Paper Comm, State Papers of Henry VIII,
Vols 1-11,
Public Record Office

Simon Thurley, *The Royal Palaces of Tudor England,*
Yale 1993

Retha Warnicke, *The Rise and Fall of Anne Boleyn,*
Canto 1991

Rosemary Weinstein, *Tudor London,*
HMSO 1994

R N Wornum, *Hans Holbein,*
Chapman Hall 1867

Most of the sites publish their own excellent handbooks which provide good visual material as well as factual information.

INDEX OF SITES

Bold numbers mark the main entry for each site.